THE LAW OF CHILD CUSTODY

by
Margaret C. Jasper

Oceana's Legal Almanac Series:
Law for the Layperson

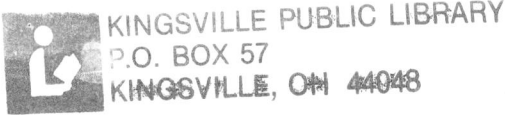
KINGSVILLE PUBLIC LIBRARY
P.O. BOX 57
KINGSVILLE, OH 44048

1997
Oceana Publications, Inc.
Dobbs Ferry, N.Y.

Information contained in this work has been obtained by Oceana Publications from sources believed to be reliable. However, neither the Publisher nor its authors guarantee the accuracy or completeness of any information published herein, and neither Oceana nor its authors shall be responsible for any errors, omissions or damages arising from the use of this information. This work is published with the understanding that Oceana and its authors are supplying information, but are not attempting to render legal or other professional services. If such services are required, the assistance of an appropriate professional should be sought.

Jasper, Margaret C.
    The Law of Child Custody / by Margaret C. Jasper.
    p. cm. — (Oceana's legal almanac series. Law for the layperson)
    Includes bibliographical references.
    ISBN: 0-379-11237-X (acid-free paper)
1. Custody of children–United States–Popular works. I. Title. II. Series.
KF547.Z9J37   1997
346.7301'73–dc21

Copyright 1997 by Oceana Publications, Inc.

All rights reserved. No part of this publication may be reproduced or transmitted in any form or by any means, electronic or mechanical, including photocopy, recording, xerography, or any information storage and retrieval system, without permission in writing from the publisher.

Manufactured in the United States of America on acid-free paper.

Legal Almanac Series
ISSN: 1075-7376

To My Husband Chris

**Your love and support
are my motivation and inspiration**

and

In memory of my son, Jimmy

ABOUT THE AUTHOR

MARGARET C. JASPER is an attorney engaged in the general practice of law in South Salem, New York, concentrating in the areas of personal injury and entertainment law. Ms. Jasper holds a Juris Doctor degree from Pace University School of Law, White Plains, New York, is a member of the New York and Connecticut bars, and is certified to practice before the United States District Courts for the Southern and Eastern Districts of New York, and the United States Supreme Court.

Ms. Jasper has been appointed to the panel of arbitrators of the American Arbitration Association and the law guardian panel for the Family Court of the State of New York, and is a New York State licensed real estate broker and member of the Westchester County Board of Realtors, operating as Jasper Real Estate, in South Salem, New York.

Ms. Jasper is the author and general editor of the following legal almanacs: Juvenile Justice and Children's Law; Marriage and Divorce; Estate Planning; The Law of Contracts; The Law of Dispute Resolution; Law for the Small Business Owner; The Law of Personal Injury; Real Estate Law for the Homeowner and Broker; Everyday Legal Forms; Dictionary of Selected Legal Terms; The Law of Medical Malpractice; The Law of Product Liability; The Law of No-Fault Insurance; The Law of Immigration; The Law of Libel and Slander; The Law of Buying and Selling; Elder Law; The Right to Die; AIDS Law; and Obscenity, Pornography and the Law.

TABLE OF CONTENTS

INTRODUCTION ix
CHAPTER 1 - HISTORICAL PERSPECTIVE 1
    The English Common Law and Colonial America 1
    The Emergence of the Tender Years Doctrine 1
    The "Best Interests of the Child" Standard 2
CHAPTER 2 - DETERMINING CUSTODY 3
    The Impact of Divorce 3
    Factors to be Considered 4
    Types of Custody Arrangements 7
CHAPTER 3 - VISITATION 11
    In General 11
    The Noncustodial Parent's Right 11
    Scheduling Visitation 12
    Age as a Factor 12
    Non-Parental Visitation Rights 13
CHAPTER 4 - INTERSTATE CUSTODY LITIGATION 15
    In General 15
    Forum Shopping 15
    Parenting Across State Lines 16
CHAPTER 5 - INTERNATIONAL CUSTODY LITIGATION . 17
    In General 17
    The Hague Convention on the Civil Aspects of International
        Child Abduction 18
    Abduction to Non-Hague Convention Member Countries . . . 19
CHAPTER 6 - CHILD ABUSE 23
    In General 23
    State Intervention 23
    Types of Abuse 24
CHAPTER 7 - CHILD SUPPORT 27
    In General 27
    Federal Child Support Guidelines 27
    Federal/State Child Support Enforcement 28
    The Federal Parent Locator Service 28
    Establishing Paternity 28

Establishing the Support Order 28
Enforcing the Support Order 29
Tax Aspects of Child Support 29

APPENDICES
  APPENDIX 1
    SAMPLE CLAUSE CONCERNING RELIGIOUS
    UPBRINGING 33
  APPENDIX 2
    SAMPLE JOINT CUSTODY AGREEMENT 35
  APPENDIX 3
    TABLE OF STATE STATUTES GOVERNING
    GRANDPARENT VISITATION 39
  APPENDIX 4
    AMERICAN BAR ASSOCIATION POLICY
    RESOLUTION ON GRANDPARENT VISITATION . . 45
  APPENDIX 5
    UNIFORM CHILD CUSTODY JURISDICTION ACT . . 47
  APPENDIX 6
    PARENTAL KIDNAPPING PREVENTION ACT OF 1980 . 57
  APPENDIX 7
    HAGUE CONVENTION ON THE CIVIL ASPECTS OF
    INTERNATIONAL CHILD ABDUCTION 61
  APPENDIX 8
    THE U.S. DEPARTMENT OF STATE APPLICATION
    FOR ASSISTANCE UNDER THE HAGUE
    CONVENTION 75
  APPENDIX 9
    DIRECTORY OF CENTRAL AUTHORITIES OF THE
    HAGUE CONVENTION CONTRACTING STATES . . 77
  APPENDIX 10
    SAMPLE WILL CLAUSE APPOINTING A
    CUSTODIAN FOR MINOR CHILDREN 79
  APPENDIX 11
    TABLE OF STATE CHILD PORNOGRAPHY
    STATUTES 81
GLOSSARY 85
BIBLIOGRAPHY 95

INTRODUCTION

One of the most difficult and painful tasks judges are asked to undertake is to determine a child custody award. The judge, a virtual stranger to the broken family, is asked to decide what is best for the innocent child when his or her mother and father wish to part. The child's psychological health tends to be overlooked by both parties.

Determining child custody is a task which most courts would rather be worked out amicably by the two adults who have created the situation. Unfortunately, given the fact that these cases are generally bitterly fought and filled with emotion, the court, as an impartial arbiter of the facts, must involve itself to protect the child.

This legal almanac explores the law of child custody. The almanac presents the history of child custody decisionmaking in the United States, and the modern-day standards by which courts make custody awards. The almanac discusses the factors a court considers in making a custody determination, and sets forth the types of custody arrangements which are available.

The difficulties related to interstate and international custody litigation and parental child abduction are also discussed, as well as the custody related topics of visitation, child support, and child abuse.

The Appendix provides tables and text of applicable statutes, and other pertinent information and data. The Glossary contains definitions of many of the terms used throughout the almanac.

CHAPTER 1:

HISTORICAL PERSPECTIVE

The English Common Law and Colonial America

Under early English common law, children were viewed primarily as a cheap source of labor. They were often sent away from their families at a very early age and placed into apprenticeship. If they resisted, they were subject to punishment, such as imprisonment or banishment. At that time, custody of the children was awarded solely to the fathers.

Many children emigrated to the colonies as part of a forced labor market, some without parents to accompany them to the New World. Treatment of children in colonial America followed the harsh English tradition. At a very young age, usually at about 10 years old, children were placed into apprenticeship or sent off to serve another family in indentured servitude.

The custody of children was largely dependent on the economic needs of the colonies. A child born out-of-wedlock, once weaned, was often taken from the mother and placed with a "master." Under common-law, neither the father nor the mother was legally entitled to custody of an illegitimate child. Slave children were subject to sale at any age.

Women had few rights under colonial law. Divorce was rare. However, if it did occur, the father had an absolute right to custody unless he was proven unfit. The underlying assumption was that fathers would be better able to financially support their children, as well as provide for their training and education in order to make them productive members of society.

If the father died, custody rights were often assigned, either by will or court order, to a male guardian. In the rare instance a mother was able to gain custody, the father was no longer obligated to financially support his children.

The Emergence of the Tender Years Doctrine

In the mid to late nineteenth century, the law was expanded to permit mothers to retain custody of children under the age of seven—the so-called *Tender Years Doctrine*. It provided for a maternal preference with respect to the custody of young children unless the mother was proven unfit.

In a drastic turnabout, the *Tender Years Doctrine* was adopted in virtually every jurisdiction, and mothers were given custody in almost all contested custody cases. This maternal preference continued to prevail in custody decisions until the mid-1980's, when a trend toward equal custody rights emerged.

The "Best Interests of the Child" Standard

Beginning with the feminist movement of the 1960's, through the next several decades, virtually all jurisdictions eliminated the maternal preference by case law or statute. The new standard to be relied on was a custody determination which was in the "best interests of the child." Theoretically, fathers—including unwed fathers—were given an equal right to obtain custody.

Although there have been rapid advances towards fair and equal determinations of custody between fathers and mothers, it should be noted that many judges still retain the notion that mothers are better caretakers of young children. This attitude is often reflected in their custody decisions.

However, if challenged, a judge's decision to give preference to a parent on the basis of sex would most likely be held unconstitutional. The "best interests of the child" standard is still followed as the standard by which judges award custody.

CHAPTER 2:

DETERMINING CUSTODY

The Impact of Divorce

When a childless marriage fails, the parties to the divorce are able to walk away from the relationship and move on with their lives. This is not possible in a divorce involving children. While divorce may end the role of spouse, it does not end the role of parent.

The impact of divorce on a child can be devastating. Divorce often results in drastic changes in the child's lifestyle. He or she must adjust to a radically different relationship with each parent. Instead of coming home to a two-parent family, time is now "scheduled" with the non-custodial parent. Family life as the child knew it is never the same.

No longer married, the parents must, for the sake of the child, maintain a certain level of amicable communication. Much of the trauma associated with divorce can be lessened, or possibly eliminated, if the parents work together to try and maintain as "normal" a life for the child as possible under the circumstances. The emotional well-being of the child following a divorce should be of paramount concern to both parents. For example, every effort must be made to resolve custody and visitation issues without involving the child.

Unfortunately, this is not always the case. Children are often used in harmful ways by one or both of the parents engaged in an adversarial divorce. For example, the child may be viewed as a convenient "bargaining chip" in divorce negotiations, particularly where financial issues are concerned. Children are often used as "spies" who must report back to the other side on what goes on in each of the households.

Bitterness between ex-spouses may lead to programming the child with negative, misleading and erroneous information about the other spouse. A common problem involves "brainwashing" of the child by one parent against the other. This destructive behavior can have devastating long-term effects on the child.

Brainwashed children may accept all of the negative programming and purposely alienate themselves from the other parent. Thus, they lose out on what would likely be a very significant factor in their overall development. They deprive themselves of a loving parent and, as a consequence, they are also deprived of the extended family attached to that parent.

A brainwashed child seeks to gain favor in the sight of the offending parent by joining in the denigration of the other parent. Unfortunately, this behavior is usually encouraged and rewarded by the offending parent. The child, however, may harbor inner feelings of guilt and anxiety. Whether purposeful or unconscious, this type of behavior must be stopped to avoid irreparable psychological harm. If necessary, a change of physical custody and therapeutic intervention to "de-program" the child may be the only solution.

Whatever differences the adults may have with each other, this kind of activity confuses and further burdens the child who is already devastated by the breakup of the family unit. The best interests of the child should always be in the forefront to prevent irreparable psychological damage that will stay with the child on into adulthood, and carry over into his or her own parenting behavior.

In general, development of a "positive" post-divorce situation includes the involvement of—and cooperation between—both parents in the day-to-day life of the child. This includes the absence of parental conflict, maintenance of stability and consistency in both households, and the involvement of the extended family.

Factors to be Considered

Although the rules vary from state to state, most courts determining child custody take into account certain factors and generally award custody according to the standard known as "the best interests of the child."

There are a number of factors which a Court considers in reaching a custody decision, including: (i) the emotional ties between the parent and child; (ii) the mental and physical fitness of the parent; (iii) the parent's ability to provide a stable and nurturing environment for the child; (iv) the parental preference of a child who is of sufficient age and maturity; and (v) the willingness of the proposed custodial parent to cooperate in encouraging a good relationship between the child and the noncustodial parent.

In addition, the court may order a home study and/or psychological evaluation of the parties and the child, before making a custody determination. In many jurisdictions, the court may appoint a law guardian—an attorney for the child—who makes an impartial determination as to which parent would make the better custodian of the child.

The courts no longer use the financial ability of a parent as a basis for awarding custody. Instead, child support and property distribution awards are used to ensure that the custodial parent has adequate means to financially support the child.

The information sought by the Court in making a custody determination is often introduced through the testimony and reports of child psychologists, social service workers, the parents, witnesses, and the children themselves. Some of the major factors considered by the Court in awarding custody are discussed in more detail below.

Child's Preference

The courts struggle with the amount of weight to be given a child's preference when it comes to a custody decision. For example, a child may simply prefer to live with the more "lenient" parent, which may not always be in the child's best interests.

The court will usually meet with the child "in camera"—i.e., in the judge's chambers. The child will often be interviewed privately by the judge so that he or she can determine, by experience, whether the child's preference—particularly the very young child—is the result of programming by one parent.

The child's age and maturity are factors to be considered. For example, an older child's preference may be given greater weight. It is recognized that teenagers often make their own custody decisions "with their feet," and it is nearly impossible to force a teenager to stay with one parent against his or her will.

Religious Issues

There are many contested issues involved in child custody litigation. Reaching a decision may be further complicated when the religious upbringing of the child becomes an issue in the dispute.

Controversy over the religious upbringing of a child introduces constitutional considerations into the proceedings. The court is called upon to balance the religious rights of the parents and child, while constrained by the Fourteenth Amendment which makes applicable to the state judiciary the First Amendment to the United States Constitution. The First Amendment prohibits the making of law respecting an establishment of religion, or prohibiting its free exercise.

The court is clearly not permitted to favor one religion over another in making a custody determination. However, the court may consider whether a particular religion maintains practices which are harmful to the child. Further, a court may consider whether a particular religion has been an important factor in the child's life, and whether such continuity is in the best interests of the child. This does not require the court to make a value judgment concerning any particular religion.

In general, a custodial parent in a sole custody situation has the right to determine the child's religious upbringing. However, this does not preclude the noncustodial parent from exposing the child to his or her religion, unless there is some indication of harm to the child. This reasoning would likely be followed in joint custody situations where the parents are unable to cooperate in a decision on the child's religious upbringing. Parents may also agree, in writing, as to the religious upbringing of the child.

A sample clause concerning the religious upbringing of a child is set forth in the Appendix.

Psychological Evaluation

At the beginning of a custody dispute, the court usually appoints an independent psychologist to assist in determining the custody arrangement. The court-appointed psychologist is not hired by either parent, therefore, his or her recommendation is likely to be impartial.

In addition to a psychological evaluation of the child, the court will often request an evaluation of all persons who participate in the caretaking of the child. This includes the parents, stepparents, and may also include grandparents or other family members who are in close day-to-day contact with the child.

A psychological evaluation may include: (i) testing; (ii) behavioral observation; (iii) interviews; and (iv) an investigation into areas which explore the parent's overall stability, such as the parent's willingness to cooperate with the other parent; his or her relationship to the child; and his or her availability for the child's day-to-day needs, etc. A review of relevant records, such as school records, police records, medical records, and any past psychological treatment may also be helpful in reaching a determination.

The attorneys for the parents may also bring in their own expert witness psychologist to promote their position and render a second opinion. A parent who disagrees with the recommendations of the court-appointed psychologist will likely bring in his or her own expert to rebut any adverse testimony of the court-appointed psychologist. However, the fact that the retained expert is compensated by a litigant lessens the impact of the testimony which is often perceived as biased.

A psychologist is under an ethical duty to avoid situations which involve or give the appearance of a conflict of interest. For example, the court-appointed psychologist owes a duty to the court to render a recommendation which is solely focused on the best interests of the child. If the same psychologist were also the treating therapist for one of the litigants, this would create a dual relationship which would endanger the impartiality of the psychologist in rendering his or her recommendation.

Nevertheless, in the above scenario, once the litigation has been concluded, the dual relationship is ended and the psychologist may take the role as the treating therapist for one or more of the parties. However, he or she is thereafter ethically prohibited from resuming his or her role as the independent evaluator in any future custody litigation involving the same parties.

Types of Custody Arrangements

There are a number of custody arrangements which the parents can maintain following a divorce. If the parents can amicably agree to work out child custody issues in a reasonable manner, without court intervention, the child will be able to move on with the adjustments that much sooner. Litigation creates a bitter atmosphere and clouds what should truly be the most important issue—the happiness and emotional health of the child.

In the unfortunate event that the parents cannot amicably agree to a reasonable custody arrangement, the dispute must be settled in court. However, custody litigation should be avoided if at all possible, and reserved only for those instances where a child's welfare would be seriously endangered by living with a parent who is clearly unfit.

The three most common types of custody arrangements are sole custody, joint custody, and split custody.

Sole Custody

Sole custody exists when one parent is designated the custodial parent—i.e., the parent who takes care of the basic daily needs of the child. The sole custodial parent also has the right to make all of the decisions concerning the child, including those decisions affecting the child's education and health. He or she is under no obligation to consult with the other parent before making such decisions.

In a sole custody situation, the child lives with the custodial parent. Although the noncustodial parent does not relinquish parenthood, his or her role is severely limited and consists mainly of visits with the child. If the noncustodial parent was previously very involved in the child's daily upbringing, sole custody presents a drastic change for both child and parent. Nevertheless, it is important that the noncustodial parent maintain as close a relationship with the child as possible under the circumstances, e.g. regular telephone contact, in order to lessen the emotional impact of such a loss.

Joint Custody

Joint custody exists when both parents legally share responsibility for the child. Although the living arrangements may be similar to that of a sole custody situation, joint custody implies that both parents are entitled to take equal responsibility for any decisions affecting the child. Such decisions may involve medical, educational and religious issues. Of course, to succeed, the parties to the joint custody arrangement must be able to cooperate with each other.

In working out a joint custody arrangement, efforts may be made to more evenly divide the child's time with each parent. For example, the child may be in the physical custody of the mother during weekdays and in the physical custody of the father during weekends, or the child may spend alternating weeks with each parent.

For an example of joint custody scheduling, see the sample joint custody agreement set forth in the Appendix.

In some situations, it is the parents who agree to "move" in and out of the house, and the child maintains his or her residence in the former marital home. In this way, the child's life is not as severely disrupted as a result of the differences which separated the adults.

In any event, there are a variety of ways in which living arrangements can be worked out as long as the parents are dedicated to making joint custody work. Of course, such a schedule also necessitates that the parents live within a reasonable distance from each other.

The ability of the parents to cooperate with each other is a priority consideration of the court in granting joint custody. If the parents are unable to put their differences aside and recognize that it is the child's interests which must remain in the forefront, a joint custody arrangement simply will not work.

Split Custody

In families where there is more than one child, split custody may be an alternative—i.e., each party may take custody of one or more of the children. For example, the boys may live with the father, and the girls may live with the mother.

However, courts are generally not in favor of splitting up siblings, based on a general belief that it is best for children of the same family to grow up together. This is particularly so following a divorce, because siblings can be a great source of stability and comfort to one another.

Although sibling splitting is generally discouraged, split custody may be awarded when it is in a child's best interests. This may occur when the children have developed separate and distinct parental attachments, or where it is clearly one child's preference to be with the "other" parent.

CHAPTER 3:

VISITATION

In General

Part of a custody determination is to decide where the child will maintain his or her primary physical residence. This is required except in the rare instances where the parents agree to move in and out of the house, leaving the child's home life substantially intact, as discussed in Chapter 2.

The physical custody of the child is often a "sticking point" in reaching a custody agreement. Often, this is due to the fact that the physical custodian, as primary caretaker of the child, is usually awarded child support to be paid by the noncustodial parent. In many cases, custody litigation begins after the parties are unable to agree to child support issues. The topic of child support is discussed in more detail in Chapter 7.

The Noncustodial Parent's Right

When one parent is designated the primary physical custodian of the child, the other parent—the "noncustodial parent"—is given what are commonly known as "visitation" rights. Unless the parents are so cooperative that they are able to enjoy flexible visitation "as the parties may agree," the court will order a visitation schedule, which may be quite detailed.

A visitation schedule is usually ordered even when joint custody is awarded. However, the schedule is usually worded so as to avoid making one parent feel like a "visitor." The schedule is often written in terms of which parent will have "physical custody" of the child on such and such dates.

In almost all cases, the noncustodial parent has an absolute right to visitation with the child. If the custodial parent maliciously or willfully interferes with that right, some jurisdictions will use this interference as a basis to transfer physical custody to the other parent.

In addition, attempts by the custodial parent to move the child out of the jurisdiction, thereby cutting off the noncustodial parent's visitation rights, will be seriously scrutinized. Most jurisdictions have carefully defined the limited circumstances under which the custodial parent is permitted to move when such a move threatens the visitation rights of the noncustodial parent.

Of course, the court cannot restrict the relocation of the custodial parent, but it can transfer custody of the child to the noncustodial parent if the custodial parent insists on relocating. Further, if the custody agreement restricts relocation, the court will most likely uphold the terms of the agreement. The courts generally find that continued contact with both parents is in the best interests of the child and should be maintained.

The relationship between the noncustodial parent and the child is a very important factor considered by the Court, such that visitation is generally denied only in cases where the noncustodial parent is clearly a danger to the child. Nevertheless, even in those cases a Court will often grant supervised visitation.

Scheduling Visitation

Ideally, the parents should be able to work out a suitable and mutually convenient visitation schedule without court intervention. Again, however, this is often not the case, particularly in situations following a bitter divorce. Parents bent on disagreement often argue about the most minute details of the visitation schedule, e.g., pick-up and drop-off times.

In those situations where the parents clearly cannot agree, the court is called upon to order a visitation schedule. The order will often detail exact dates and times for weekly, holiday and vacation visitation to take place.

Age as a Factor

The length and frequency of visitation with the noncustodial parent is often dependent upon, among other factors, the age of the child. The general consensus is that children under five years of age are best suited to consistent, frequent visits with the noncustodial parent, particularly when the child has strongly bonded with the parent.

It has been suggested, however, that the younger child preferably maintain the consistency of sleeping in his or her own crib until approximately two years of age, in order to make the child feel more secure in his or her surroundings. As the child matures, overnight visits can be introduced at longer and more frequent intervals.

School-age children usually participate in extracurricular activities and develop friendships among their peers. At this age, a balance must be reached between allowing the child to maintain a normal social life versus "sticking to" the visitation schedule. Flexibility is often the preferred route to take to avoid putting pressure on the child to "make the choice." Parents who are able to cooperate with each other will likely be able to work around an active child's schedule. It is important, however, to maintain consistent telephone contact when physical visitation is limited.

Once a child reaches adolescence, given the likelihood of a very active social life, it is unlikely that any scheduled visitation will work if it interferes with their plans. Again, flexibility, an "open-door policy," and frequent telephone contact will help to maintain a strong parent-child bond.

Non-Parental Visitation Rights

Children form strong bonds with many people during the course of their lives. When their family unit is disrupted, either by divorce or death, their relationship with various other family members is also radically altered.

It is important for parents to recognize that depriving a child of a significant relationship may be emotionally damaging. It is an additional loss that the child must suffer, and to which he or she must adjust.

Every effort should be made to allow the child to maintain significant relationships even if the parent through whom the child developed such a relationship is no longer in the child's life. Although this may be at times inconvenient or undesirable, one must remember that it is not the child's fault that the adults are unable to work out their differences.

The most significant of such relationships involve extended family members, such as grandparents, and stepparents and stepsiblings.

Grandparent Visitation

Grandparents have the legal right to petition a court for visitation privileges with their grandchildren. It has been recognized that grandparents play a very important role in a child's development. Of course, it is important that the grandparent does not take an active role in the dispute between the parents.

This may be difficult because the grandparent will obviously be concerned about his or her own child. However, if the grandparent is to play a positive role in the child's life, particularly during a difficult divorce, it is crucial that he or she remain impartial and avoid involving the child in the dispute. Any negative views the grandparent may hold about the other parent should not be shared with the child or the grandparent may risk losing visitation privileges.

Some of the factors courts consider in awarding visitation privileges to a grandparent include: (i) the nature of the existing relationship between the grandparent and child; (ii) the effect of such visitation on the child's relationship with his or her parents; (iii) the child's wishes in maintaining a relationship with his or her grandparent; and (iv) the effect of such visitation on the child's emotional development.

A table of state statutes governing grandparent visitation, and the text of the American Bar Association Policy Resolution on Grandparent Visitation is set forth in the Appendix.

CHAPTER 4:

INTERSTATE CUSTODY LITIGATION

In General

A parent may be confronted with having to deal with child custody issues across state lines—interstate—or with a foreign country. These issues usually arise when the custodial parent relocates, either with court permission or in defiance of a court order.

As the "missing children" hotlines and milk carton advertisements demonstrate, an overwhelming number of parents choose to flee with their children rather than allow the courts to determine custody.

A parent often removes a child and drops out of sight completely. Of course, this causes the abandoned parent immense pain and suffering, as well as the financial burden of trying to locate the child and/or litigate in a foreign jurisdiction, i.e. another state or country. This is particularly difficult where the parent has relocated to a foreign country. International custody litigation is discussed more fully in Chapter 5.

Forum Shopping

It is often the absconding parent's intention to relocate in a jurisdiction which he or she feels will render a more favorable determination than would have been made in the home state. Of course, this also creates an extreme hardship and disadvantage for the other parent who must litigate custody in a distant jurisdiction.

The Uniform Child Custody Jurisdiction Act (UCCJA) and the Parental Kidnapping Prevention Act (PKPA) were promulgated to combat the serious problem of jurisdictional conflict and parental forum shopping in custody decisions.

The Uniform Child Custody Jurisdiction Act

The Uniform Child Custody Jurisdiction Act of 1968 (UCCJA) has been adopted by all of the states and the District of Columbia. The UCCJA's goal is to eliminate the motives for forum shopping among the states, and to encourage cooperation between the state courts.

The UCCJA sets forth the requirements a particular jurisdiction must meet in order to make a custody determination when two states are involved. The law also requires both jurisdictions to cooperate in determining the proper forum in which to resolve the custody dispute.

When the courts of two different states are in conflict, the UCCJA provides that a federal court can rule as to which state is the proper forum in which to litigate custody. The federal court will not, however, decide the merits of a custody dispute.

The statute favors awarding jurisdiction to the child's home state, thus deterring parental forum shopping and child snatching. Further, the UCCJA prohibits a state from exercising jurisdiction in a custody action if another state's court has already been involved in the case.

The Uniform Child Custody Jurisdiction Act is set forth in the Appendix.

The Parental Kidnapping Prevention Act

The Parental Kidnapping Prevention Act of 1980 (PKPA) requires the appropriate authorities of every state to enforce custody and visitation orders made by courts having proper jurisdiction. The PKPA also authorizes the Federal Parental Locator Service to locate children who have been abducted by a parent. Thus, when a parent removes a child from a jurisdiction against court order or contrary to a custody agreement, the lawful custodial parent can obtain federal assistance in locating the child.

In many jurisdictions, the parent who wrongfully takes the child is subject to criminal sanctions for abducting the child and interfering with custody. Under the PKPA, the Fugitive Felon Act applies to state felony cases involving parental kidnapping and interstate or international flight to avoid prosecution. In such a case, a request for a Federal Unlawful Flight to Avoid Prosecution (UFAP) warrant may be filed with the local U.S. Attorney's Office by the state prosecutor.

Relevant provisions of The Parental Kidnapping Prevention Act are set forth in the Appendix.

Parenting Across State Lines

Once jurisdiction has been established in another state, the noncustodial parent necessarily suffers a type of forced exile from his or her child. In those cases, the courts often attempt to fashion a remedy which will assist the noncustodial parent in maintaining a meaningful relationship with the child.

For example, the noncustodial parent may be awarded expanded visitation privileges, such as more holiday visits, or entire summers, etc. This expansion of visitation is crucial to maintain a strong parent-child bond, particularly because visits during the school year will necessarily be limited if the distance between the custodial and noncustodial home is significant.

CHAPTER 5:

INTERNATIONAL CUSTODY LITIGATION

In General

International parental child abduction has become a serious problem in the last several decades. This is due in large part to the relative ease of international travel, and the increase in cross-cultural marriages.

The outcome of a custody dispute which crosses international boundaries depends largely on the country to which the parent relocates. One must deal with the complexities of foreign law and the large expense of having to litigate one's case in a foreign country, where he or she may be confronted with cultural bias favoring the absconding parent with close ties to the country.

There are a number of precautions one may take if they are in a cross-cultural marriage and they fear the possibility that their child is vulnerable to abduction. A child is particularly vulnerable if there is trouble in the marriage, or an impending divorce, and the other parent has close ties with a foreign country. In order to prepare for the possibility of an abduction, the United States Department of State has suggested the following precautions:

1. Realize that voluntary travel to the foreign country may result in the child being prevented from returning to the United States. Some foreign countries prohibit travel by a child and/or a woman without the husband's permission. It is crucial that one inquire about all of the applicable laws and cultural traditions before traveling abroad.

2. Compile information about the other parent to be used in case of an abduction. Keep names and addresses of friends and relatives in the United States and in the foreign country. Maintain a record of the other parent's personal data, such as passport number, social security number, and driver's license number, etc.

3. Keep an up-to-date written and detailed description of your child and take color photographs every six months. This information will be very helpful in locating the child if the need should arise.

4. Teach your child what to do in case he or she is removed from the country. For example, teach your child how to use a telephone to call for help.

5. If you are separated or divorced, it is best to obtain a custody decree which incorporates a provision prohibiting your child from traveling out of the United States without your permission. Provide certified copies of the decree to any persons who may be responsible for your child, such as

the school, daycare center, and babysitter, etc. Alert them to the possibility that an abduction may take place and instruct them to contact you if there are any unscheduled attempts to retrieve the child.

The Hague Convention on the Civil Aspects of International Child Abduction

In General

The Hague Convention on the Civil Aspects of International Child Abduction (the "Hague Convention"), adopted by the Hague Conference in 1980, has attempted to combat the problem of international parental child abduction.

The Hague Convention's objective is to resolve problems related to international parental child abduction among its member nations by making sure such children are immediately returned to their country of origin. The member nations are referred to in the Convention as "contracting states."

The text of the Hague Convention is set forth in the Appendix.

In 1988, the United States became a party to the Hague Convention, and implemented legislation providing for the commencement of international child custody litigation under federal law. Its provisions largely mirror the UCCJA and provide procedures for filing international petitions seeking the return of a child, visitation rights, and habeas corpus proceedings.

A copy of the United States Department of State Application for Assistance Under the Hague Convention on Child Abduction is set forth in the Appendix.

As of 1993, thirty countries had become signatories to the Hague Convention. They include Argentina (1991); Australia (1987); Austria (1988); Belize (1989); Burkina Faso (1992); Canada (1983); Croatia (former Yugoslavia) (1991); Denmark (1991); Ecuador (1992); France (1983); Germany (1990); Greece (1993); Hungary (1986); Ireland (1991); Israel (1991); Luxembourg (1987); Mauritius (1992); Mexico (1991); Monaco (1992); Netherlands (1990); New Zealand (1991); Norway (1989); Poland (1991); Portugal (1983); Romania (1993); Spain (1987); Sweden (1989); Switzerland (1984); United Kingdom (1986); and The United States (1988).

Central Authorities

As set forth in Article 6 of the Convention, each contracting state must designate a Central Authority to handle complaints of child abduction, and to cooperate with the Central Authorities of other contracting states to carry out the objectives of the Convention, i.e., secure the prompt return of abducted children. The duties of the **Central** Authorities in carrying out this objective include:

1. Discovering the whereabouts of the abducted child;

2. Taking such measures necessary to prevent further harm to the child;

3. Securing the voluntary return of the child and amicably resolving the issues;

4. Exchanging information concerning the child;

5. Providing general information concerning its own law as it pertains to the Convention;

6. Initiating judicial or administrative proceedings necessary to secure the return of the child;

7. Providing legal aid and advice to the parties;

8. Providing administrative arrangements necessary to secure the return of the child; and

9. Keeping each other informed and eliminating obstacles which would hinder carrying out the objective of the Convention.

If you suspect that your child has been abducted to a country that is a party to the Hague Convention, you should contact the Office of Citizens Consular Services (CCS) in Washington, D.C. CCS is the designated Central Authority for the United States.

A Directory of the Central Authorities of each of the contracting states is set forth in the Appendix.

Abduction to Non-Hague Convention Member Countries

In General

If the foreign country to which your child is abducted is not a party to the Hague Convention, you can seek legal remedies against the absconding parent in the federal civil and criminal court systems. Once you suspect that an abduction has occurred, there are a number of steps you can take to locate your child and press charges against the abducting parent:

1. If you have not already done so, seek a custody decree that prohibits your child from traveling without your permission. Without a custody decree granting you sole custody of the child, you will not have legal standing to bring an action.

2. File a missing person report with the local police department and the National Center for Missing and Exploited Children, and request that the Federal Parent Locator Service attempt a search for the absconding parent.

3. Request the Department of State's Office of Citizen's Consular Services (CCS) to initiate a welfare and whereabouts search for your child overseas.

4. Inform the embassy and consulates of the country to which you suspect your child has been taken of your custody decree. Instruct them not to issue a foreign passport or visa to your child.

5. Check the U.S. Passport Agency to see whether a passport has been issued in your child's name.

6. If your child is school-age, contact his or her school officials and ask to be informed if anyone requests a transfer of your child's records.

7. Try and track down the absconding parent through personal contacts and records, e.g., friends and relatives, and credit card and telephone bills.

8. Once your child has been located, retain an attorney in the foreign jurisdiction.

9. Seek to have an arrest warrant under state and/or federal statutes issued for the arrest of the absconding parent.

10. Once the arrest warrant has been issued, have the absconding parent's name registered with the National Crime Information Center and, if a U.S. citizen, seek to have his or her passport revoked. Consider whether extradition would be possible.

Application of the UCCJA and PKPA to International Abduction Cases

Section 23 of the Uniform Child Custody Jurisdiction Act ("UCCJA"), although not intentionally drafted to meet the needs of international custody disputes, does provide for international application. The Parental Kidnapping Prevention Act ("PKPA") may also provide additional remedies.

Again, see the relevant provisions of the Uniform Child Custody Jurisdiction Act and the Parental Kidnapping Prevention Act set forth in the Appendix.

Civil Remedies

As set forth above, you should first obtain a custody decree. Although it has no binding legal force in the foreign country, it may be persuasive, depending on the country and its relationship with the United States. If the foreign jurisdiction is one which holds a cultural or gender bias, it may be more difficult to regain the child. The absconding parent may have the advantage in the court of his or her own country, particularly if that country is biased in favor of one gender as caretaker of the child. Again, it is recommended that one retain a lawyer in the foreign country who is familiar with its laws and traditions.

Criminal Remedies

The United States Department of State has advised that formal resort to the criminal justice system should be a last resort. It may force the absconding parent to go deeper into hiding with the child. Further, such action is not likely to result in the extradition of the absconding parent to the United States, and may only serve to delay or complicate the return of your child, which is your immediate objective.

Nevertheless, if you have no other choice, there are certain steps which must be followed. You, or your lawyer, must contact the appropriate law enforcement authorities to request that an arrest warrant be issued for the absconding parent.

The issuance of a Federal Unlawful Flight to Avoid Prosecution (UFAP) warrant pursuant to the Federal Parental Kidnapping Prevention Act can be requested from the FBI or your state Attorney General. The warrant serves two purposes. It alerts the foreign country that the abduction was illegal and that the absconding parent is considered a federal fugitive under the law of the United States. Further, it may compel the absconding parent to return the child voluntarily, particularly if he or she expects to return to the United States for business or other reasons.

CHAPTER 6:

CHILD ABUSE

In General

Allegations of some type of child abuse by one parent against the other often accompany modern-day child custody litigation. Such allegations may involve physical, emotional or sexual abuse. Unfortunately, some parents use the immoral tactic of making false allegations to gain an advantage in the litigation.

Of course, the mere allegation of child abuse is disturbing and, once made, is difficult to retract. This is particularly destructive when the false allegation is one of sexual abuse. When such an allegation is made, the accused parent is usually deprived of contact with the child until a full investigation is conducted.

Meanwhile, the child is subjected to a series of tests exploring sexual issues, and the accused parent is unfairly embarrassed by having to defend against such an allegation. To make matters worse, there have been a number of instances where testing results in a contradictory result, or a false positive indication of sexual abuse. It is certainly known to be a difficult determination to make.

A child who has been subjected to abuse—physical, emotional or sexual—must be protected at all costs. That is why such an allegation must be thoroughly explored and either confirmed or ruled out. This is so whether the abuser is a parent, another family member or a stranger.

The abuse or neglect of a child by one or both parents is a major factor considered by the court in awarding custody and granting visitation rights. For example, if it is shown that a noncustodial parent has abused the child, depending on the type and extent of such abuse, efforts may be made to have visitation supervised. In more serious cases, a petition may be brought to have the parental rights of the offender terminated.

State Intervention

When both parents are guilty of abuse and/or neglect, the state, in its role as *parens patriae*, may step in and take custody of the child. This also occurs when a child is abandoned or orphaned. When the state intervenes in such situations, attempts are generally made to place the child with relatives.

In the case of the death of a surviving parent, the will of the deceased may appoint a person to take custody of the minor child. If there are no relatives or appointees willing or available to take custody of the child, the state will provide living arrangements for the child. The child may be placed in a private foster home or a group home, many of which are owned and operated by the private sector or religious organizations. Efforts may be made to place a child—particularly a younger child or infant—for adoption.

A sample will provision appointing a custodian for one's minor children is set forth in the Appendix.

Types of Abuse

Abuse takes many forms. As set forth in *The Child Abuse Prevention Treatment Act*, child abuse and neglect involves "the physical or mental injury (sexual abuse or exploitation, negligent treatment or maltreatment) of a child (a person under the age of 18, unless the child protection law of that state in which the child resides specifies a younger age for cases not involving sexual abuse) by a person (including any employee of a residential facility or any staff personnel providing out-of-home care) who is responsible for the child's welfare under circumstances which indicate that the child's health or welfare is harmed or threatened thereby. . ."

A discussion of the most common ways in which a child suffers abuse is set forth below.

Physical Abuse

The Child Abuse Prevention Treatment Act defines physical abuse as "inflicting physical injury by punching, beating, kicking, biting, burning, or otherwise harming a child." Such injuries may have been unintentional, e.g. having resulted from excessive physical punishment.

Studies have shown that parents who suffered abuse as children often repeat this behavior with their own children. Further, parents who suffer from drug or alcohol addiction are more likely to abuse their children. Abuse has also been found to exist to a greater degree when the home environment is under stress, e.g. a single-parent household, or a household suffering from depressed financial conditions, etc.

Neglect

The Child Abuse Prevention Treatment Act defines child neglect as "the failure to provide the child's basic needs." This would include physical, educational or emotional needs, for example, the failure to seek necessary health care for a sick child, or the failure to enroll a school-age child in an educational program. The factors which indicate the likelihood of physical abuse in a particular household are substantially the same for child neglect.

Emotional Abuse

It is often the case that a child's emotional well-being is ignored provided that he or she appears to be physically well cared for. However, the reality is that emotional abuse of a child often carries much deeper and longlasting scars than a physical beating. Some examples of emotional abuse which negatively impair a child's psychological health include: (i) constant verbal assault on the child; (ii) rejection; (iii) punishment involving close confinement; and (iv) the threat of physical harm. Children who have suffered psychological mistreatment are often characterized by low self-esteem and aggressive or other socially inappropriate behavior.

Studies have shown that parents who suffered emotional neglect as children often repeat this behavior with their own children. Drug and alcohol addiction, a stressful home environment and the mental state of the parent are also known to contribute to this problem.

Sexual Abuse

Child sexual abuse has been defined by the U.S. Department of Health and Human Services to include "fondling a child's genitals, intercourse, incest, rape, sodomy, exhibitionism and the sexual exploitation of a child." It is incomprehensible that parents may be responsible for involving their young children in the child pornography industry for financial gain. Nevertheless, it is a daily occurrence.

Child pornography and prostitution are highly organized, multi-million dollar industries that operate in our society on a nationwide scale. Sadly, parents often serve as perpetrators of this crime against their own children. In 1977, Congressional hearings were held on the subject of child pornography, also known as "kiddie porn." Witnesses who appeared before Congress told nightmare tales about small children who were kidnapped by pornographers, or sold to pornographers by their parents.

Outraged federal and state legislators have since attempted to enact laws to combat this widespread problem. Following the 1977 Congressional hearings, two federal statutes were passed. First enacted was *The Protection of Children from Sexual Exploitation Act of 1977* which prohibits the production of any sexually explicit material using a child under the age of sixteen, if such material is destined for, or has already traveled in interstate commerce.

In response to allegations that children were being sold by their parents into the pornography industry, the law was made applicable to parents or other custodians who knowingly permit a child to participate in the production of sexually explicit material.

Subsequently, greater enforcement was obtained by enacting *The Child Protection Act of 1984* which eliminated the requirement that child pornography distribution be undertaken for the purpose of "sale," and raised the age of protection to eighteen. In addition, penalties under the 1984 Act were greatly increased over those set forth in the 1977 Act, and a provision for criminal and civil forfeiture was included.

A table of state child pornography statutes is set forth in the Appendix.

The child victims of sexual exploitation and sexual abuse, in general, come from a wide variety of family backgrounds, including all socioeconomic classes and religions. They range in age from infancy through adolescence. Young children are often victimized by someone they know, e.g. a neighbor or family member. Many crave adult affection, and are lured into the behavior in an effort to obtain approval by adult authority figures.

The long-term effects on children who have been victims of sexual abuse are devastating. They are generally unable to form normal sexual relationships with persons of the opposite sex. Many child victims fall into destructive lifestyles, such as drug and alcohol addiction, and many succumb to suicide.

CHAPTER 7:

CHILD SUPPORT

In General

Child support is the payment of money from one parent to another for the maintenance of the child or children of that relationship, whether or not the parties to the relationship were ever married. The payment of child support is usually made to the custodial parent—the parent with whom the child legally resides—by the noncustodial parent.

The terms of the child support award can be agreed upon by the parties, as long as the custodial parent is made aware of the amount the child may be entitled to under the law. The agreement must be fair to all parties and in the best interests of the child. Upon application to a court, the parent can have the agreement converted into an enforceable legal order. If the parties cannot agree to a support amount, then the decision will be made by the court after a formal hearing.

The payment of child support is a legal obligation which continues until either the child is emancipated or the obligated parent dies. Emancipation occurs when the child reaches the age of majority, which is usually eighteen but extends until the age of twenty-one in some states. In addition, a child may be emancipated if he or she marries, joins the armed services, or otherwise voluntarily leaves the care and control of the custodial parent. However, emancipation does not necessarily occur just because a child physically leaves the custodial parent's household, such as for the purpose of attending school.

Federal Child Support Guidelines

In 1989, the federal government enacted child support guidelines which each state is mandated to use in determining the amount of child support orders in cases where the parties cannot mutually agree to support amounts. The child support guidelines set forth a formula, based on such factors as parental income and the number of children for whom support is sought, in order to arrive at the support amount. The child support guidelines must be used unless it can be shown that to use them would be unjust or inappropriate in a particular case. If a court departs from using the guidelines in any case, it must give its reasons, on the record, for its decision.

Federal/State Child Support Enforcement

The federal government requires the states to implement enforcement programs to ensure that child support is paid. The child support enforcement program is usually handled by the state's child support enforcement office in conjunction with the domestic relations or family court of the jurisdiction.

The enforcement program assists the custodial parent in locating an absent non-paying parent, establishing paternity, establishing the support order, and collecting and enforcing the child support order.

The Federal Parent Locator Service

The federal government has established the Federal Parent Locator Service (FPLS), which uses information contained in federal records, such as Internal Revenue Service files, Social Security files, and Veterans Administration files, to locate absent parents. In addition, each state has established a State Parent Locator Service (SPLS), which uses state records, such as Department of Motor Vehicles files and state unemployment insurance files, to locate absent parents.

Establishing Paternity

When the parents of a child were never married, the paternity of the child must be established before an order of support can be made. If the father does not object to paternity, he can sign a written admission of paternity, which can be filed with the court. However, if the father is contesting paternity, the matter must be decided by a court.

Evidence, such as blood and genetic tests, will be produced to support the paternity petition. Once paternity is established, the child is legally entitled to the same rights and privileges as a child born of married parents, including the right to support, inheritance, and other benefits.

Establishing the Support Order

After the noncustodial parent is located, an enforceable support order must be established. Most states use administrative procedures to expedite the establishment of a legally binding support order. If the parties agree to the amount of support, the agreement can be made into a legally enforceable order of support as long as it conforms to certain requirements of fairness.

If the parties cannot agree, a hearing is conducted to establish the terms of the support order. Depending on the laws of the particular state, support awards can be increased or decreased if one of the parties seeks modification of the order. The ability to modify a support order depends on certain factors, as set forth by the state, which may include a change in circumstances of the parties, such as a loss of employment, or a change in the needs of the child.

Enforcing the Support Order

In recognition of the need for strict enforcement of child support orders, the federal government has implemented a variety of rules for the collection of child support. The states are obligated to follow those directives. For example, as of January 1994, all child support orders are subject to immediate wage withholding unless both parents and/or the court agree to a different plan.

Presently, wage withholding only applies to new child support enforcement cases, or for existing cases, at the request of either parent, as long as the state agrees. A noncustodial parent can also request his or her employer to make automatic payroll deductions for child support, and the employer is required, under federal law, to comply with this request.

When the noncustodial parent is self-employed, or otherwise not easily subject to wage withholding, and reneges on his or her obligation to pay child support, other enforcement action can be taken. Such action may include placing liens on the real or personal property of the debtor parent or intercepting the federal or state income tax refunds of the debtor parent. In addition, child support arrears may be reported to consumer credit agencies.

States are also required to vigorously pursue the enforcement of child support orders against out-of-state noncustodial parents. Each state has its own form of interstate enforcement legislation, such as the Uniform Reciprocal Enforcement of Support Act (URESA), which provides for the enforcement of support orders across state lines.

Tax Aspects of Child Support

Child support is not considered income to the parent who receives the payments and is not deductible from the taxable income of the paying parent. In order to claim a child as a dependent, a parent must contribute more than fifty percent of the child's total support. Generally, the custodial parent may claim the exemption. However, the parents may agree otherwise. If the custodial parent assigns the exemption, in writing, to the noncustodial parent, the noncustodial parent can claim the exemption on his or her tax return.

APPENDICES

APPENDIX 1:

SAMPLE CLAUSE CONCERNING RELIGIOUS UPBRINGING

The parties agree that, in order to maintain the continuity of the child's religious affiliation and education, the child will be brought up in the Catholic faith and will continue to attend St. Joan of Arc Elementary School, or in the event that the child shall relocate out of the parish of said school, the child will attend the Catholic parochial school of the parish which serves the child's new home.

APPENDIX 2:

SAMPLE JOINT CUSTODY AGREEMENT

THIS AGREEMENT, made this___day of_____, 1997, by and between JOHN SMITH, residing at 123 Main Street, White Plains, New York (hereinafter referred to as "Father") and MARY SMITH, residing at 456 Elm Street, White Plains, New York (hereinafter referred to as "Mother"),

WITNESSETH :

WHEREAS, the parties were divorced on the 31st day of December, 1995, in the City of White Plains, County of Westchester, in the State of New York; and

WHEREAS, there is one child born of the marriage, to wit: JOSEPH SMITH, age 10, born on September 19, 1987 (hereinafter referred to as "the child"); and

WHEREAS, the parties desire to resolve the custody arrangements of their minor child;

NOW THEREFORE, in consideration of the promises and undertakings herein set forth both parties do hereby covenant and agree as follows:

1. Father and Mother shall have joint legal custody of their minor child and equal input into all matters relating to the child's health, education and welfare.

2. Father is hereby designated as primary residential custodian of the child.

3. Father shall not relocate the child from the State of New York. If Father desires to relocate outside of the State of New York, Mother shall become the primary residential custodian of the child.

4. Father and Mother agree to share physical custody of the child according to the following schedule:

(a) Every Wednesday throughout the year, except as may conflict with the holiday schedule as set forth in (c) below, the child shall be in the physical custody of the Mother, who will pick up the child at 5:30 p.m., and return the child the following morning at 8:00 a.m., for his timely delivery by Mother to school, or on non-school days, to the custodial residence.

(b) Every other weekend throughout the year, except as may conflict with the holiday schedule as set forth in (c) below, the child shall be in the physical custody of the Mother, who will pick up the child at 5:30 p.m. on Friday, and return the child at 8:00 a.m. on Monday morning, for his timely delivery by Mother to school, or on non-school days, to the custodial residence.

(c) The following holiday schedule shall take precedence over the above regular schedule:

(i) On holidays which fall on a Monday, the child shall remain with the parent who has had the child for that weekend. If the child is in the physical custody of Mother, Mother shall return the child at 8:00 a.m. on Tuesday morning, for his timely delivery by Mother to school, or on non-school days, to the custodial residence.

(ii) Effective as of the date of this Agreement, the child shall spend alternating Thanksgiving Holidays with the Mother in odd-numbered years and the Father in even-numbered years.

(iii) Effective as of the date of this Agreement, the child shall spend alternating Easter Holidays with the Mother in even-numbered years and the Father in odd-numbered years.

(iv) Effective as of the date of this Agreement, the child shall spend alternating Christmas Eve Holidays with the Mother in odd-numbered years and the Father in even-numbered years, beginning at 3:00 p.m. on December 24th through 10:00 a.m. on December 25th.

(v) Effective as of the date of this Agreement, the child shall spend alternating Christmas Day Holidays with the Mother in even-numbered years and the Father in odd-numbered years, beginning at 10:00 a.m. on December 25th through December 26th at 10:00 a.m.

(d) The parties agree to the following vacation schedule:

(i) Each party is entitled to physical custody of the child for one-half of the summer vacation, with the dates to be established no later than May 31st.

(ii) Each party is entitled to physical custody of the child for one-half of the designated spring recess, with the dates and times to be agreed to between the parties.

(iii) Each party is entitled to physical custody of the child for one-half of the designated winter recess, with the dates and times to be agreed to between the parties.

APPENDIX 2

5. The parties may, upon mutual agreement, amend the above schedule to accommodate the demands of work, illness, school schedules, or for other good cause.

IN WITNESS WHEREOF, the parties have signed, sealed and acknowledged this Agreement as of the date first written above.

_____

JOHN SMITH

_____

MARY SMITH

STATE OF NEW YORK)

COUNTY OF WESTCHESTER)

On the ___ day of _____, 1997, before me personally came JOHN SMITH and MARY SMITH, to me known and known to me to be the individuals described in and who executed the foregoing instrument, and who acknowledged to me that they executed the same.

_____

NOTARY PUBLIC

APPENDIX 3:

TABLE OF STATE STATUTES GOVERNING GRANDPARENT VISITATION

STATE	STATUTE	GENERAL PROVISIONS
Alabama	Alabama Code §30-3-3	Upon death of parent (child of grandparent) or during divorce, separation, annulment or child custody proceedings between parents.
Alaska	Alaska Statutes §25.24.150	Upon death of parent (child of grandparent) or during divorce, separation, annulment or child custody proceedings between parents.
Arizona	Arizona Revised Statutes Annotated §25-337.01	Upon death of parent (child of grandparent) or during divorce, separation, annulment or child custody proceedings between parents.
Arkansas	Arkansas Statutes Annotated §9-13-103	Upon death of parent (child of grandparent) or during divorce, separation, annulment or child custody proceedings between parents.
California	California Civil Code §§197.5; 4601	Upon death of parent (child of grandparent)
Colorado	Colorado Revised Statutes §19-1-116	Upon death of parent (child of grandparent) or during divorce, separation, annulment or child custody proceedings between parents.
Connecticut	Connecticut General Statutes Annotated 6646b-59-59a	Circumstances under which grandparent visitation could be obtained are unspecified.
Delaware	Delaware Code Annotated, Title 10, §950(7)	During divorce, separation, annulment or child custody proceedings between parents.
Florida	Florida Statutes §61.13(2); (b)2c	During divorce, separation, annulment or child custody proceedings between parents.
Georgia	Georgia Code Annotated §19-7-3	Upon death of parent (child of grandparent).
Hawaii	Hawaii Revised Statutes §571.46(7)	During divorce, separation, annulment or child custody proceedings between parents.
Idaho	Idaho Code §32-1008	Circumstances under which grandparent visitation could be obtained is unspecified.

STATE	STATUTE	GENERAL PROVISIONS
Illinois	Illinois Annotated Statutes, Chapter 40, §607(b)(c)	Upon death of parent (child of grandparent) or during divorce, separation, annulment or child custody proceedings between parents.
Indiana	Indiana Code Annotated §§31-1-11.7-1 to 7-8	Upon death of parent (child of grandparent) or during divorce, separation, annulment or child custody proceedings between parents.
Iowa	Iowa Code Annotated §§598.35-36	Upon death of parent (child of grandparent) or during divorce, separation, annulment or child custody proceedings between parents.
Kansas	Kansas Statutes Annotated §60-1616(b)	Circumstances under which grandparent visitation could be obtained are unspecified.
Kentucky	Kentucky Revised Statutes Annotated §405.021	Circumstances under which grandparent visitation could be obtained are unspecified.
Louisiana	Louisiana Revised Statutes Annotated §9:572	Upon death of parent (child of grandparent) or during divorce, separation, annulment or child custody proceedings between parents.
Maine	Maine Revised Statutes Annotated, Title 19 §752	Circumstances under which grandparent visitation could be obtained are unspecified.
Maryland	Maryland Family Law Code Annotated §9-102	During divorce, separation, annulment or child custody proceedings between parents.
Massachusetts	Massachusetts General Laws Annotated, Chapter 119 §39D	Upon death of parent (child of grandparent) or during divorce, separation, annulment or child custody proceedings between parents.
Michigan	Michigan Compiled Laws Annotated §722.72(b)	Upon death of parent (child of grandparent) or during divorce, separation, annulment or child custody proceedings between parents.
Minnesota	Minnesota Statutes Annotated §257.022	Upon death of parent (child of grandparent) or during divorce, separation, annulment or child custody proceedings between parents; or depending on the amount of time child lived with grandparent.
Mississippi	Mississippi Code Annotated §§93-16-1	Upon death of parent (child of grandparent) or during divorce, separation, annulment or child custody proceedings between parents.

APPENDIX 3

STATE	STATUTE	GENERAL PROVISIONS
Missouri	Missouri Annotated Statutes §§452.400-4-2	Upon death of parent (child of grandparent) or during divorce, separation, annulment or child custody proceedings between parents.
Montana	Montana Code Annotated §§40-9-101-102	Circumstances under which grandparent visitation could be obtained are unspecified.
Nebraska	Nebraska Revised Statutes §§43-1801-1803	Upon death of parent (child of grandparent) or during divorce, separation, annulment or child custody proceedings between parents.
Nevada	Nevada Revised Statutes §§125A.330-340	Upon death of parent (child of grandparent) or during divorce, separation, annulment or child custody proceedings between parents.
New Hampshire	New Hampshire Revised Statutes Annotated §458:17	During divorce, separation, annulment or child custody proceedings between parents.
New Jersey	New Jersey Statutes Annotated §9:2-7.1	Upon death of parent (child of grandparent) or during divorce, separation, annulment or child custody proceedings between parents.
New Mexico	New Mexico Statutes Annotated §§40-9-1 to 4	Upon death of parent (child of grandparent) or during divorce, separation, annulment or child custody proceedings between parents.
New York	New York Domestic Relations Law §§72, 240(1)	Upon death of parent (child of grandparent) or during divorce, separation, annulment or child custody proceedings between parents, other circumstances under which grandparent visitation could be obtained are unspecified.
North Carolina	North Carolina General Statutes §§50-13.2(b), 2A, 5(j)	During divorce, separation, annulment or child custody proceedings between parents.
North Dakota	North Dakota Cent. Code §14-09-05.1	Circumstances under which grandparent visitation could be obtained are unspecified.
Ohio	Ohio Revised Code Annotated §3109.05(B)	During divorce, separation, annulment or child custody proceedings between parents.
Oklahoma	Oklahoma Statutes Annotated, Title 10 §5	Upon death of parent (child of grandparent) or during divorce, separation, annulment or child custody proceedings between parents; or depending on the amount of time child lived with grandparent.

STATE	STATUTE	GENERAL PROVISIONS
Oregon	Oregon Revised Statutes §§109.121-123	Upon death of parent (child of grandparent) or during divorce, separation, annulment or child custody proceedings between parents.
Pennsylvania	23 Pennsylvania Cons. Statutes Annotated §§5311-5314	Upon death of parent (child of grandparent) or depending on the amount of time child lived with grandparent.
Rhode Island	Rhode Island General Laws §§15-5-24.1-2	Upon death of parent (child of grandparent) or during divorce, separation, annulment or child custody proceedings between parents.
South Carolina	South Carolina Code Annotated §20-7-420(33)	Circumstances under which grandparent visitation could be obtained are unspecified.
South Dakota	South Dakota Codified Laws Annotated §§25-4-52 to 54	Upon death of parent (child of grandparent) or during divorce, separation, annulment or child custody proceedings between parents.
Tennessee	Tennessee Code Annotated §36-6-3-1	Circumstances under which grandparent visitation could be obtained are unspecified.
Texas	Texas Family code Annotated §14.03(e)-(g)	Upon death of parent (child of grandparent) or during divorce, separation, annulment or child custody proceedings between parents; or depending on the amount of time child lived with grandparent.
Utah	Utah Code Annotated §30-3-5(4)-(7)	Circumstances under which grandparent visitation could be obtained are unspecified.
Vermont	Vermont Statutes Annotated, Title 15 §§1011-1016	Upon death of parent (child of grandparent) or during divorce, separation, annulment or child custody proceedings between parents.
Virginia	Virginia Code Annotated §20-107.2	During divorce, separation, annulment or child custody proceedings between parents.
Washington	Washington Revised Code Annotated §26.09.240	Circumstances under which grandparent visitation could be obtained are unspecified.
West Virginia	West Virginia Code §§48-2-15(b)(1)	Upon death of parent (child of grandparent) or during divorce, separation, annulment or child custody proceedings between parents.

APPENDIX 3

STATE	STATUTE	GENERAL PROVISIONS
Wisconsin	Wisconsin Statutes Annotated §767.245	Circumstances under which grandparent visitation could be obtained are unspecified.
Wyoming	Wyoming Statutes §20-2-113(c)	Upon death of parent (child of grandparent) or during divorce, separation, annulment or child custody proceedings between parents.

APPENDIX 4:

AMERICAN BAR ASSOCIATION POLICY RESOLUTION ON GRANDPARENT VISITATION

RECOMMENDATION

Be it resolved that the American Bar Association encourages the further development of state law on grandparent visitation in accordance with the following guidelines:

1. Attorneys, court personnel and other professionals should be encouraged to refer persons involved in grandparent visitation disputes to appropriate mediation services. If possible such referrals should be made prior to the filing of any court action. Such mediation services should strive to develop agreements between the disputants regarding grandparent visitation, to reduce acrimony between the parties and to minimize any trauma for the child involved.

2. If the parties to a grandparent visitation dispute are unable to resolve the dispute prior to filing a court action, judges presiding in such cases should be encouraged to refer the parties to mediation. Such referrals to mediation should be made, upon motion by a party or sua sponte, if the judge determines that mediation may result in a satisfactory settlement of the dispute.

3. State legislatures should enumerate specific factors for courts to consider in determining whether grandparent visitation is in a child's best interest, including such factors as the following:

   (a) The nature and quality of the relationship between the grandparent and the child, including such factors as whether emotional bonds have been established and whether the grandparent has enhanced or interfered with the parent-child relationship;

   (b) Whether visitation will promote or disrupt the child's psychological development;

   (c) Whether visitation will create friction between the child and his or her parent(s);

   (d) Whether visitation will provide support and stability for the child after a nuclear family disruption;

   (e) The capacity of the adults involved for future compromise and cooperation in matters involving the child;

(f) The child's wishes, if the child is able to freely form and express a preference; and

(g) Any other factor relevant to a fair and just determination regarding visitation.

State legislation or court rules should require judges presiding in grandparent visitation cases to appoint qualified guardians ad litem for the children involved in such disputes.

APPENDIX 5:

UNIFORM CHILD CUSTODY JURISDICTION ACT

SECTION 1. Purposes of Act; Construction of Provisions.

(a) The general purposes of this Act are to:

(1) avoid jurisdictional competition and conflict with courts of other states in matters of child custody which have in the past resulted in the shifting of children from state to state with harmful effects on their well-being;

(2) promote cooperation with the courts of other states to the end that a custody decree is rendered in that state which can best decide the case in the interest of the child;

(3) assure that litigation concerning the custody of a child take place ordinarily in the state with which the child and his family have the closest connection and where significant evidence concerning his care, protection, training, and personal relationships is most readily available, and the courts of this state decline the exercise of jurisdiction when the child and his family have a closer connection with another state;

(4) discourage continuing controversies over child custody in the interest of greater stability of home environment and of secure family relationships for the child;

(5) deter abductions and other unilateral removals of children undertaken to obtain custody awards;

(6) avoid re-litigation of custody decisions of other states in this state insofar as feasible;

(7) facilitate the enforcement of custody decrees of other states;

(8) promote and expand the exchange of information and other forms of mutual assistance between the courts of this state and those of other states concerned with the same child; and

(9) make uniform the law of those states which enact it.

(b) this Act shall be construed to promote the general purposes stated in this section.

SECTION 2. Definitions. As used in this Act:

(1) "contestant" means a person, including a parent, who claims a right to custody or visitation rights with respect to a child;

(2) "custody determination" means a court decision and court orders and instructions providing for the custody of a child, including visitation rights; it does not include a decision relating to child support or any other monetary obligation of any person;

(3) "custody proceeding" includes proceedings in which a custody determination is one of several issues, such as an action for divorce or separation, and includes child neglect and dependency proceedings;

(4) "decree" or "custody decree" means a custody determination contained in a judicial decree or order made in a custody proceeding, and includes an initial decree and a modification decree;

(5) "home state" means the state in which the child immediately preceding the time involved lived with his parents, a parent, or a person acting as parent, for at least 6 consecutive months, and in the case of a child less than 6 months old the state in which the child lived from birth with any of the persons mentioned. Periods of temporary absence of any of the named persons are counted as part of the 6-month or other period;

(6) "initial decree" means the first custody decree concerning a particular child;

(7) "modification decree" means a custody decree which modifies or replaces a prior decree, whether made by the court which rendered the prior decree or by another court;

(8) "physical custody" means actual possession and control of a child;

(9) "person acting as parent" means a person, other than a parent, who has physical custody of a child and who has either been awarded custody by a court or claims a right to custody; and

(10) "state" means any state, territory, or possession of the United States, the Commonwealth of Puerto Rico, and the District of Columbia.

SECTION 7. Inconvenient Forum.

(a) A court which has jurisdiction under this Act to make an initial or modification decree may decline to exercise its jurisdiction any time before making a decree if it finds that it is an inconvenient forum to make a custody determination under the circumstances of the case and that a court of another State is a more appropriate forum;

(b) A finding of inconvenient forum may be made upon the court's own motion or upon motion of a party or a guardian ad litem or other representative of the child;

(c) In determining if it is an inconvenient forum, the court shall consider if it is in the interest of the child that another state assume jurisdiction. For this purpose it may take into account the following factors, among others:

(1) if another state is or recently was the child's home state;

(2) if another state has a closer connection with the child and his family or with the child and one or more of the contestants;

(3) if substantial evidence concerning the child's present or future care, protection, training, and personal relationships is more readily available in another state;

(4) if the parties have agreed on another forum which is no less appropriate; and

(5) if the exercise of jurisdiction by a court of this State would contravene any of the purposes stated in section 1.

(d) Before determining whether to decline or retain jurisdiction the court may communicate with a court of another state and exchange information pertinent to the assumption of jurisdiction by either court with a view to assuring that jurisdiction will be exercised by the appropriate court and that a forum will be available to the parties.

(e) If the court finds that it is an inconvenient forum and that a court of another state is a more appropriate forum, it may dismiss the proceedings, or it may stay the proceedings upon condition that a custody proceeding be promptly commenced in another named state or upon any other conditions which may be just and proper; including the condition that a moving party stipulate his consent and submission to the jurisdiction of the other forum.

(f) The court may decline to exercise its jurisdiction under this Act if a custody determination is incidental to on action for divorce or another proceeding while retaining jurisdiction of the other forum.

(g) If it appears to the court that it is clearly an inappropriate forum it may require the party who commenced the proceedings to pay, in addition to the costs of the proceedings in this State, necessary travel and other expenses, including attorney's fees, incurred by other parties or their witnesses. Payment is to be made to the clerk of the court for remittance to the proper party.

(h) Upon dismissal or stay of proceedings under this section the court shall inform the court found to be the more appropriate forum of this fact, or if the court which would have jurisdiction in the other state is not certainly known, shall transmit the information to the court administrator or other appropriate official for forwarding to the appropriate party.

(i) Any communication received from another state informing this State of a finding of inconvenient forum because this State is the more appropriate forum shall be filed in the custody registry of the appropriate court. Upon assuming jurisdiction the court of this State shall inform the original court of this fact.

SECTION 8. Jurisdiction Declined by Reason of Conduct.

(a) If the petitioner for an initial decree has wrongfully taken the child from another state or has engaged in similar reprehensible conduct the court may decline to exercise jurisdiction if this is just and proper under the circumstances.

(b) Unless required in the interest of the child, the court shall not exercise its jurisdiction to modify a custody decree of another state if the petitioner, without consent of the person entitled to custody, has improperly removed the child from the physical custody of the person entitled to custody or has improperly retained the child after a visit or other temporary relinquishment of physical custody. If the petitioner has violated any other provision of a custody decree of another state the court may decline to exercise its jurisdiction if this is just and proper under the circumstances.

(c) In appropriate cases a court dismissing a petition under this section may charge the petitioner with necessary travel and other expenses, including attorney's fees, incurred by other parties or their witnesses.

SECTION 9. Information under Oath to be Submitted to the Court.

(a) Every party in a custody proceeding in his first pleading or in an affidavit attached to that pleading shall give information under oath as to the child's present address, the places where the child has lived within the last 5 years, and the names and present addresses of the person with whom the child has lived during that period. In this pleading or affidavit every party shall further declare under oath whether:

(1) he has participated (as a party, witness, or in any other capacity) in any other litigation concerning the custody of the same child in this or any other state;

(2) he has information of any custody proceeding concerning the child pending in a court of this or any other state; and

(3) he knows of any person not a party to the proceedings who has physical custody of the child or claims to have custody or visitation with respect to the child.

(b) If the declaration as to any of the above items is in the affirmative the declarant shall give additional information under oath as to details of the information furnished and as to other matters pertinent to the court's jurisdiction and the disposition of the case.

(c) Each party has a continuing duty to inform the court of any custody proceeding concerning the child in this or any other state of which he obtained information during this proceeding.

SECTION 10. Additional Parties.

If the court learns from information furnished by the parties pursuant to section 9 or from other sources that a person not a party to the custody proceeding has physical custody of the child or claims to have custody or visitation rights with respect to the child, it shall order that person to be joined as a party and to be duly notified of the pendency of the proceeding and of his joinder as a party. If the person joined as a party is outside this State he shall be served with process or otherwise notified in accordance with section 5.

SECTION 11. Appearance of Parties and the Child.

(a) The court may order any party to the proceeding who is in this State to appear personally before the court. If that party has physical custody of the child the court may order that he appear personally with the child.

(b) If a party to the proceeding whose presence is desired by the court is outside this State with or without the child the court may order that the notice given under section 5 include a statement directing that party to appear personally with or without the child declaring that failure to appear may result in a decision adverse to that party.

(c) If a party to the proceeding who is outside this State is directed to appear under subsection (b) or desires to appear personally before the court with or without the child, the court may require another party to pay to the clerk of the court travel and other necessary expenses of the party so appearing and of the child if this is just and proper under the circumstances.

SECTION 12. Binding Force and Res Judicata Effect of Custody Decree.

A custody decree rendered by a court of this State which had jurisdiction under section 3 binds all parties who have been served in this State or notified in accordance with section 5 or who have submitted to the jurisdiction of the court, and who have been given an opportunity to be heard. As to these parties the custody decree is conclusive as to all issues of law and fact decided and as to the custody determination made unless and until that determination is modified pursuant to law, including the provisions of this Act.

SECTION 13. Recognition of Out-of-State Custody Decree.

The courts of this State shall recognize and enforce an initial or modification decree of a court of another state which had assumed jurisdiction under statutory provisions substantially in accordance with this Act or which was made under factual circumstances meeting the jurisdiction standards of the Act, so long as this decree has not been modified in accordance with jurisdictional standards substantially similar to those of this Act.

SECTION 14. Modification of Custody Decree of Another State.

(a) If a court of another state has made a custody decree, a court of this State shall not modify that decree unless (1) it appears to the court of this State that the court which rendered the decree does not now have jurisdiction under jurisdictional prerequisites substantially in accordance with this Act or has declined to assume jurisdiction to modify the decree and (2) the court of this State has jurisdiction.

(b) If a court of this State is authorized under subsection (a) and section 8 to modify a custody decree of another state it shall give due consideration to the transcript of the record and other documents of all previous proceedings submitted to it in accordance with section 22.

SECTION 15. Filing and Enforcement of Custody Decree of Another State.

(a) A certified copy of a custody decree of another state may be filed in the office of the clerk of any [District Court, Family Court] of this State. The clerk shall treat the decree in the same manner as a custody decree of the [District Court, Family Court] of this State. A custody decree so filed has the same effect and shall be enforced in like manner as a custody decree rendered by a court of this State.

(b) A person violating a custody decree of another state which makes it necessary to enforce the decree in this State may be required to pay necessary travel and other expenses, including attorneys' fees, incurred by the party entitled to the custody or his witnesses.

SECTION 16. Registry of Out-of-State Custody Decrees and Proceedings.

The clerk of each [District Court, Family Court] shall maintain a registry in which he shall enter the following:

(1) certified copies of custody decrees of other states received for filing;

(2) communications as to the pendency of custody proceedings in other states;

(3) communications concerning a finding of inconvenient forum by a court of another state; and

(4) other communications or documents concerning custody proceedings in another state which may affect the jurisdiction of a court of this State or the disposition to be made by it in a custody proceeding.

SECTION 17. Certified Copies of Custody Decree.

The Clerk of the [District Court, Family Court] of this State, at the request of the court of another state or at the request of any person who is affected by or has a legitimate interest in a custody decree, shall certify and forward a copy of the decree to that court or person.

SECTION 18. Taking Testimony in Another State.

In addition to other procedural devices available to a party, any party to the proceeding or a guardian ad litem or other representative of the child may adduce testimony of witnesses, including parties and the child, by deposition or otherwise, in another state. The court on its own motion may direct that the testimony of a person be taken in another state and may prescribe the manner in which and the terms upon which the testimony shall be taken.

SECTION 19. Hearing and Studies in Another State; Orders to Appeal.

(a) A court of this State may request the appropriate court of another state to hold a hearing to adduce evidence, to order a party to produce or give evidence under other procedures of that state, or to have social studies made with respect to the custody of a child involved in proceedings pending in the court of this State; and to forward to the court of this State certified copies of the transcript of the record of the hearing, the evidence otherwise adduced, or any social studies prepared in compliance with the request. The cost of the services may be assessed against the parties or if necessary, ordered paid by the [County, State].

(b) A court of this State may request the appropriate court of another state to order a party to custody proceedings pending in the court of this State to appear in the proceedings, and if that party has physical custody of the child, to appear with the child. The request may state that travel and other necessary expenses of the party and of the child whose appearance is desired will be assessed against another party or will otherwise be paid.

SECTION 20. Assistance to Courts of Other States.

(a) Upon request of the court of another state the courts of this State which are competent to hear custody matters may offer a person in this State to appear at a hearing to adduce evidence or to produce or give evidence under other procedures available in this State [or may order social studies to be made for use in a custody proceeding in another state]. A certified copy of the transcript of the record of the hearing or the evidence otherwise adduced [and any social studies prepared] shall be forwarded by the clerk of the court to the requesting court.

(b) A person within this State may voluntarily give his testimony or statement in this State for use in a custody proceeding outside this State.

(c) Upon request of the court of another state a competent court of this State may order a person in this State to appear alone or with the child in a custody proceeding in another state. The court may condition compliance with the request upon assurance by the other state that state travel and other necessary expenses will be advanced or reimbursed.

SECTION 21. Preservation of Documents for Use in Other States.

In any custody proceeding in this State the court shall preserve the pleadings, orders and decrees, any record that has been made of its hearing, social studies, and other pertinent documents until the child reaches [18, 21] years of age. Upon appropriate request of the court of another state the court shall forward to the other court certified copies of any or all of such documents.

SECTION 22. Request for Court Records of Another State.

If a custody decree has been rendered in another state concerning a child involved in a custody proceeding pending in a court of this State, the court of this State upon taking jurisdiction of the case shall request of the court record and other documents mentioned in section 21.

SECTION 23. International Application.

The general policies of this Act extend to the international area. The provisions of this Act relating to the recognition and enforcement of custody decrees of other states apply to custody decrees and decrees involving legal institutions similar in nature to custody institutions rendered by appropriate authorities of other nations if reasonable notice and opportunity to be heard were given to all affected persons.

SECTION 24. Priority.

Upon the request of a party to a custody proceeding which raises a question of existence or exercise of jurisdiction under this Act the case shall be given calendar priority and handled expeditiously.

SECTION 25. Severability.

If any provisions of this Act or the application thereof to any person or circumstance is held invalid, its invalidity does not affect other provisions or applications of the Act which can be given effect without the invalid provision or application, and to this end the provisions of this Act are severable.

SECTION 26. Short Title.

This Act may be cited as the Uniform Child Custody Jurisdiction Act.

SECTION 27. Repeal.

The following acts and parts of acts are repealed:

SECTION 28. Time of Taking Effect.

APPENDIX 6:

PARENTAL KIDNAPPING PREVENTION ACT OF 1980

28 U.S.C. 1738A. FULL FAITH AND CREDIT GIVEN TO CHILD CUSTODY DETERMINATIONS

(a) The appropriate authorities of every State shall enforce according to its terms, and shall not modify except as provided in subsection (f) of this section, any child custody determination made consistently with the provisions of this section by a court of another State.

(b) As used in this section, the term—

(1) "child" means a person under the age of eighteen;

(2) "contestant" means a person, including a parent, who claims a right to custody or visitation of a child;

(3) "custody determination" means a judgment, decree, or other order of a court providing for the custody or visitation of a child, and includes permanent and temporary orders, and initial orders and modifications;

(4) "home State" means the State in which, immediately preceding the time involved, the child lived with his parents, a parent, or a person acting as parent, for at least six consecutive months, and in the case of a child less than six months old, the State in which the child lived from birth with any of such persons. Periods of temporary absence of any of such persons are counted as part of the six-month or other period;

(5) "modification" and "modify" refer to a custody determination which modifies, replaces, supersedes, or otherwise is made subsequent to, a prior custody determination concerning the same child, whether made by the same court or not;

(6) "person acting as a parent" means a person, other than a parent, who has physical custody of a child and who has either been awarded custody by a court or claims a right to custody;

(7) "physical custody" means actual possession and control of a child; and

(8) "State" means a State of the United States, the District of Columbia, the Commonwealth of Puerto Rico, or a territory or possession of the United States.

(c) A child custody determination made by a court of a State is consistent with the provisions of this section only if-

(1) such court has jurisdiction under the law of such State; and

(2) one of the following conditions is met:

(A) such State (i) is the home State of the child on the date of the commencement of the proceeding, or (ii) had been the child's home State within six months before the date of the commencement of the proceeding and the child is absent from such State because of his removal or retention by a contestant or for other reasons, and a contestant continues to live in such State;

(B)(i) it appears that no other State would have jurisdiction under subparagraph (A), and (ii) it is in the best interest of the child that a court of such State assume jurisdiction because (I) the child and his parents, or the child and at least one contestant, have a significant connection with such State other than mere physical presence in such State and (II) there is available in such state substantial evidence concerning the child's present or future care, protection, training, and personal relationships;

(C) the child is physically present in such State and (i) the child has been abandoned, or (ii) it is necessary in an emergency to protect the child because he has been subjected to or threatened with mistreatment or abuse;

(D) (i) it appears that no other State would have jurisdiction under subparagraph (A), (B), (C), or (E), or another State has declined to exercise jurisdiction on the ground that the State whose jurisdiction is in issue is the more appropriate forum to determine the custody of the child, and (ii) it is in the best interest of the child that such court assume jurisdiction; or

(E) the court has continuing jurisdiction pursuant to subsection (d).

(d) The jurisdiction of a court of a State which has made a custody determination consistently with the provisions of this section continues as long as the requirement of subsection (c)(l) continues to be met and such State remains the residence of the child or of any contestant.

(e) Before a child custody determination is made, reasonable notice and opportunity to be heard shall be given to the contestants, any parent whose parental rights have not been previously terminated and any person who has physical custody of a child.

(f) A court of a State may modify a determination of the custody of the same child made by a court of another State, if-

(1) it has jurisdiction to make a child custody determination; and

(2) the court of the other State no longer has jurisdiction, or it has declined to exercise such jurisdiction to modify such determination.

(g) A court of a State shall not exercise jurisdiction in any proceeding for a custody determination commenced during the pendency of a proceeding in a court of another State where such court of that other State is exercising jurisdiction consistently with the provisions of this section to make a custody determination.

APPENDIX 7:

HAGUE CONVENTION ON THE CIVIL ASPECTS OF INTERNATIONAL CHILD ABDUCTION

The States signatory to the present Convention, firmly convinced that the interests of children are of paramount importance in matters relating to their custody, desiring to protect children internationally from the harmful effects of their wrongful removal or retention and to establish procedures to ensure their prompt return to the State of their habitual residence, as well as to secure protection for rights of access, have resolved to conclude a Convention to this effect, and have agreed upon the following provisions—

CHAPTER I - SCOPE OF THE CONVENTION

Article 1

The objects of the present Convention are—

(a) to secure the prompt return of children wrongfully removed to or retained in any Contracting State; and

(b) to ensure that rights of custody and of access under the law of one Contracting State are effectively respected in other Contracting States.

Article 2

Contracting States shall take all appropriate measures to secure within their territories the implementation of the objects of the Convention. For this purpose they shall use the most expeditious procedures available.

Article 3

The removal or the retention of a child is to be considered wrongful where—

(a) it is in breach of rights of custody attributed to a person, an institution or any other body, either jointly or alone, under the law of the State in which the child was habitually resident immediately before the removal or retention; and

(b) at the time of removal or retention those rights were actually exercised, either jointly or alone, or would have been so exercised but for the removal or retention. The rights of custody mentioned in sub-paragraph a above, may arise in particular by operation of law or by reason of a judicial or administrative decision, or by reason of an agreement having legal effect under the law of that State.

Article 4

The Convention shall apply to any child who was habitually resident in a Contracting State immediately before any breach of custody or access rights. The Convention shall cease to apply when the child attains the age of 16 years.

Article 5

For the purposes of this Convention—

(a) "rights of custody" shall include rights relating to the care of the person of the child and, in particular, the right to determine the child's place of residence;

(b) "rights of access" shall include the right to take a child for a limited period of time to a place other than the child's habitual residence.

CHAPTER II - CENTRAL AUTHORITIES

Article 6

A Contracting State shall designate a Central Authority to discharge the duties which are imposed by the Convention upon such authorities. Federal States, States with more than one system of law or States having autonomous territorial organizations shall be free to appoint more than one Central Authority and to specify the territorial extent of their powers. Where a State has appointed more than one Central Authority, it shall designate the Central Authority to which applications may be addressed for transmission to the appropriate Central Authority within that State.

Article 7

Central Authorities shall co-operate with each other and promote co-operation amongst the competent authorities in their respective States to secure the prompt return of children and to achieve the other objects of this Convention. In particular, either directly or through any intermediary, they shall take all appropriate measures—

(a) to discover the whereabouts of a child who has been wrongfully removed or retained;

(b) to prevent further harm to the child or prejudice to interested parties by taking or causing to be taken provisional measures;

(c) to secure the voluntary return of the child or to bring about an amicable resolution of the issues;

(d) to exchange, where desirable, information relating to the social background of the child;

(e) to provide information of a general character as to the law of their State in connection with the application of the Convention;

(f) to initiate or facilitate the institution of judicial or administrative proceedings with a view to obtaining the return of the child and, in a proper case, to make arrangements for organizing or securing the effective exercise of rights of access;

(g) where the circumstances so require, to provide or facilitate the provision of legal aid and advice, including the participation of legal counsel and advisers;

(h) to provide such administrative arrangements as may be necessary and appropriate to secure the safe return of the child;

(i) to keep other each other informed with respect to the operation of this Convention and, as far as possible, to eliminate any obstacles to its application.

CHAPTER III - RETURN OF CHILDREN

Article 8

Any person, institution or other body claiming that a child has been removed or retained in breach of custody rights may apply either to the Central Authority of the child's habitual residence or to the Central Authority of any other Contracting State for assistance in securing the return of the child.

The application shall contain—

(a) information concerning the identity of the applicant, of the child and of the person alleged to have removed or retained the child;

(b) where available, the date of birth of the child;

(c) the grounds on which the applicant's claim for return of the child is based;

(d) all available information relating to the whereabouts of the child and the identity of the person with whom the child is presumed to be.

The application may be accompanied or supplemented by—

(e) an authenticated copy of any relevant decision or agreement;

(f) a certificate or an affidavit emanating from a Central Authority, or other competent authority of the State of the child's habitual residence, or from a qualified person, concerning the relevant law of that State;

(g) any other relevant document.

Article 9

If the Central Authority which receives an application referred to in Article 8 has reason to believe that the child is in another Contracting State, it shall directly and without delay transmit the application to the Central Authority of that Contracting State and inform the requesting Central Authority, or the applicant, as the case may be.

Article 10

The Central Authority of the State where the child is shall take or cause to be taken all appropriate measures in order to obtain the voluntary return of the child.

Article 11

The judicial or administrative authorities of Contracting States shall act expeditiously in proceedings for the return of children.

If the judicial or administrative authority concerned has not reached a decision within six weeks from the date of commencement of the proceedings, the applicant or the Central Authority of the requested State, on its own initiative or if asked by the Central Authority of the requesting State, shall have the right to request a statement of the reasons for the delay. If a reply is received by the Central Authority of the requested State, that Authority shall transmit the reply to the Central Authority of the requesting State, or to the applicant, as the case may be.

Article 12

Where a child has been wrongfully removed or retained in terms of Article 3 and, at the date of the commencement of the proceedings before the judicial or administrative authority of the Contracting State where the child is, a period of less than one year has elapsed from the date of the wrongful removal or retention, the authority concerned shall order the return of the child forthwith.

The judicial or administrative authority, even where the proceedings have been commenced after the expiration of the period of one year referred to in the preceding paragraph, shall also order the return of the child, unless it is demonstrated that the child is now settled in its new environment.

Where the judicial or administrative authority in the requested State has reason to believe that the child has been taken to another State, it may stay the proceedings or dismiss the application for the return of the child.

Article 13

Notwithstanding the provisions of the preceding Article, the judicial or administrative authority of the requested State is not bound to order the return of the child if the person, institution or other body which opposes its return establishes that—

>   (a) the person, institution or other body having the care of the person of the child was not actually exercising the custody rights at the time of removal or retention, or had consented to or subsequently acquiesced in the removal of retention; or

>   (b) there is a grave risk that his or her return would expose the child to physical or psychological harm or otherwise place the child in an intolerable situation.

The judicial or administrative authority may also refuse to order the return of the child if it finds that the child objects to being returned and has attained an age and degree of maturity at which it is appropriate to take account of its views.

In considering the circumstances referred to in this Article, the judicial and administrative authorities shall take into account the information relating to the social background of the child provided by the Central Authority or other competent authority of the child's habitual residence.

Article 14

In ascertaining whether there has been a wrongful removal of retention within the meaning of Article 3, the judicial or administrative authorities of the requested State may take notice directly of the law of, and of judicial or administrative decisions, formally recognized or not in the State of the habitual residence of the child, without recourse to the specific procedures for the proof of that law or for the recognition of foreign decisions which would otherwise be applicable.

Article 15

The judicial or administrative authorities of a Contracting State may, prior to the making of an order for the return of the child, request that the applicant obtain from the authorities of the State of the habitual residence of the child a decision or other determination that the removal or retention was wrongful within the meaning of Article 3 of the Convention, where such a decision or determination may be obtained in that State. The Central Authorities of the Contracting States shall so far as practicable assist applicants to obtain such a decision or determination.

Article 16

After receiving notice of a wrongful removal or retention of a child in the sense of Article 3, the judicial or administrative authorities of the Contracting State to which the child has been removed or in which it has been retained shall not decide on the merits of rights of custody until it has been determined that the child is not to be returned under this Convention or unless an application under the Convention is not lodged within a reasonable time following receipt of the notice.

Article 17

The sole fact that a decision relating to custody has been given in or is entitled to recognition in the requested State shall not be a ground for refusing to return a child under this Convention, but the judicial or administrative authorities of the requested State may take account of the reasons for that decision in applying this Convention.

Article 18

The provisions of this Chapter do not limit the power of a judicial or administrative authority to order the return of the child at any time.

Article 19

A decision under this Convention concerning the return of the child shall not be taken to be determinative on the merits of any custody issue.

Article 20

The return of the child under the provision of Article 12 may be refused if this would not be permitted by the fundamental principles of the requested State relating to the protection of human rights and fundamental freedoms.

CHAPTER IV - RIGHTS OF ACCESS

Article 21

An application to make arrangements for organizing or securing the effective exercise of rights of access may be presented to the Central Authorities of the Contracting States in the same way as an application for the return of a child.

The Central Authorities are bound by the obligations of co-operation which are set forth in Article 7 to promote the peaceful enjoyment of access rights and the fulfillment of any conditions to which the exercise of such rights may be subject. The Central Authorities shall take steps to remove, as far as possible, all obstacles to the exercise of such rights. The Central Authorities, either directly or through intermediaries, may initiate or assist in the institution of proceedings with a view to organizing or protecting these rights and securing respect for the conditions to which the exercise of these rights may be subject.

CHAPTER V - GENERAL PROVISIONS

Article 22

No security, bond or deposit, however described, shall be required to guarantee the payment of costs and expenses in the judicial or administrative proceedings falling within the scope of this Convention.

Article 23

No legalization or similar formality may be required in the context of this Convention.

Article 24

Any application, communication or other document sent to the Central Authority of the requested State shall be in the original language, and shall be accompanied by a translation into the official language or one of the official languages of the requested State or, where that is not feasible, a translation into French or English.

However, a Contracting State may, by making a reservation in accordance with Article 42, object to the use of either French or English, but not both, in any application, communication or other document sent to its Central Authority.

Article 25

Nationals of the Contracting States and persons who are habitually resident within those States shall be entitled in matters concerned with the application of this Convention to legal aid and advice in any other Contracting State on the same conditions as if they themselves were nationals of and habitually resident in that State.

Article 26

Each Central Authority shall bear its own costs in applying this Convention. Central Authorities and other public services of Contracting States shall not impose any charges in relation to applications submitted under this Convention. In particular, they may not require any payment from the applicant towards the costs and expenses of the proceedings or, where applicable, those arising from the participation of legal counsel or advisers.

However, they may require the payment of the expenses incurred or to be incurred in implementing the return of the child.

However, a Contracting State may, by making a reservation in accordance with Article 42, declare that it shall not be bound to assume any costs referred to in the preceding paragraph resulting from the participation of legal counsel or advisers or from court proceedings, except insofar as those costs may be covered by its system of legal aid and advice.

Upon ordering the return of a child or issuing an order concerning rights of access under this Convention, the judicial or administrative authorities may, where appropriate, direct the person who removed or retained the child, or who prevented the exercise of rights of access, to pay necessary expenses incurred by or on behalf of the applicant, including travel expenses, any costs incurred or payments made for locating the child, the costs of legal representation of the applicant, and those of returning the child.

Article 27

When it is manifest that the requirements of this Convention are not fulfilled or that the application is otherwise not well founded, a Central Authority is not bound to accept the application. In that case, the Central Authority shall forthwith inform the applicant or the Central Authority through which the application was submitted, as the case may be, of its reasons.

Article 28

A Central Authority may require that the application be accompanied by a written authorization empowering it to act on behalf of the applicant, or to designate a representative so to act.

Article 29

This Convention shall not preclude any person, institution or body who claims that there has been a breach of custody or access rights within the meaning of Article 3 or 21 from applying directly to the judicial or administrative authorities of a Contracting State, whether or not under the provisions of this Convention.

Article 30

Any application submitted to the Central Authorities or directly to the judicial or administrative authorities of a Contracting State in accordance with the terms of this Convention, together with documents and any other information appended thereto or provided by a Central Authority, shall be admissible in the courts or administrative authorities of the Contracting States.

Article 31

In relation to a State which in matters of custody of children has two or more systems of law applicable in different territorial units—

(a) any reference to habitual residence in that State shall be construed as referring to habitual residence in a territorial unit of that State;

(b) any reference to the law of the State of habitual residence shall be construed as referring to the law of the territorial unit in that State where the child habitually resides.

Article 32

In relation to a State which in matters of custody of children has two or more systems of law applicable to different categories of persons, any reference to the law of that State shall be construed as referring to the legal system specified by the law of that State.

Article 33

A State within which different territorial units have their own rules of law in respect of custody of children shall not be bound to apply this Convention where a State with a unified system of law would not be bound to do so.

Article 34

This Convention shall take priority in matters within its scope over the Convention of 5 October 1961 concerning the powers of authorities and the law applicable in respect of the protection of minors, as between Parties to both Conventions. Otherwise the present Convention shall not restrict the application of an international instrument in force between the State of origin and the State addressed or other law of the State addressed for the purposes of obtaining the return of a child who has been wrongfully removed or retained or of organizing access rights.

Article 35

This Convention shall apply as between Contracting States only to wrongful removals or retentions occurring after its entry into force in those States.

Where a declaration has been made under Article 39 or 40, the reference in the preceding paragraph to a Contracting State shall be taken to refer to the territorial unit or units in relation to which this Convention applies.

Article 36

Nothing in this Convention shall prevent two or more Contracting State, in order to limit the restrictions to which the return of the child may be subject, from agreeing among themselves to derogate from any provision of this Convention which may imply such a restriction.

CHAPTER VI - FINAL CLAUSES

Article 37

The Convention shall be open for signature by the States which were Members of the Hague Conference on Private International Law at the time of its Fourteenth Session. It shall be ratified, accepted or approved and the instruments of ratification, acceptance or approval shall be deposited with the Ministry of Foreign Affairs of the Kingdom of the Netherlands.

Article 38

Any other State may accede to the Convention. The instrument of accession shall be deposited with the Ministry of Foreign Affairs of the Kingdom of the Netherlands.

The Convention shall enter into force for a State acceding to it on the first day of the third calendar month after the deposit of its instrument of accession. The accession will have effect only as regards the relations between the acceding State and such Contracting States as will have declared their acceptance of the accession. Such a declaration will also have to be made by any Member State ratifying, accepting or approving the Convention after an accession. Such declaration shall be deposited at the Ministry of Foreign Affairs of the Kingdom of the Netherlands; this Ministry shall forward, through diplomatic channels, a certified copy to each of the Contracting States.

The Convention will enter into force as between the acceding State and the State that has declared its acceptance of the accession on the first day of the third calendar month after the deposit of the declaration of acceptance.

Article 39

Any State may, at the time of signature, ratification, acceptance, approval or accession, declare that the Convention shall extend to all the territories for the international relations of which it is responsible, or to one or more of them. Such a declaration shall take effect at the time the Convention enters into force for that State. Such declaration, as well as any subsequent extension, shall be notified to the Ministry of Foreign Affairs of the Kingdom of the Netherlands.

Article 40

If a Contracting State has two or more territorial units in which different systems of law are applicable in relation to matters dealt with in this Convention, it may at the time of signature, ratification, acceptance, approval or accession declare that this Convention shall extend to all its territorial units or only to one or more of them and may modify this declaration by submitting another declaration at any time. Any such declaration shall be notified to the Ministry of Foreign Affairs of the Kingdom of the Netherlands and shall state expressly the territorial units to which the Convention applies.

Article 41

Where a Contracting State has a system of government under which executive, judicial and legislative powers are distributed between central and other authorities within that State, its signature or ratification, acceptance or approval of, or accession to this Convention, or its making of any declaration in terms of Article 40 shall carry no implication as to the internal distribution of powers within that State.

Article 42

Any State may, not later than the time of ratification, acceptance, approval or accession, or at the time of making a declaration in terms of Article 39 or 40, make one or both of the reservations provided for in Article 24 and Article 26, third paragraph. No other reservations shall be permitted. Any State may at any time withdraw a reservation it has made. The withdraw shall be notified to the Ministry of Foreign Affairs of the Kingdom of the Netherlands. The reservation shall cease to have effect on the first day of the third calendar month after the notification referred to in the preceding paragraph.

Article 43

The Convention shall enter into force on the first day of the third calendar month after the deposit of the third instrument of ratification, acceptance, approval or accession referred to in Articles 37 and 38. Thereafter the Convention shall enter into force—

(1) for each State ratifying, accepting, approving or acceding to it subsequently, on the first day of the third calendar month after the deposit of its instrument of ratification, acceptance, approval or accession;

(2) for any territory or territorial unit to which the Convention has been extended in conformity with Article 39 or 40, on the first day of the third calendar month after the notification referred to in that Article.

Article 44

The Convention shall remain in force for five years form the date of its entry into force in accordance with the first paragraph of Article 43 even for States which subsequently have ratified, accepted, approved it or acceded to it. If there has been no denunciation, it shall be renewed tacitly every five years. Any denunciation shall be notified to the Ministry of Foreign Affairs of the Kingdom of the netherlands at least six months before the expiry of the five year period. It may be limited to certain of the territories or territorial units to which the Convention applies.

The denunciation shall have effect only as regards the State which has notified it. The Convention shall remain in force for the other Contracting States.

Article 45

The Ministry of Foreign Affairs of the Kingdom of the Netherlands shall notify the States Members of the Conference, and the States which have acceded in accordance with Article 38, of the following—

(1) the signatures and ratifications, acceptances and approvals referred to in Article 37;

(2) the accession referred to in Article 38;

(3) the date on which the Convention enters into force in accordance with Article 43;

(4) the extensions referred to in Article 39;

(5) the declarations referred to in Articles 38 and 40;

(6) the reservations referred to in Article 24 and Article 26, third paragraph, and the withdrawals referred to in Article 42;

(7) the denunciation referred to in Article 44.

In witness whereof the undersigned, being duly authorized thereto, have signed this Convention.

Done at The Hague, on the 25th day of October, 1980, in the English and French languages, both texts being equally authentic, in a single copy which shall be deposited in the archives of the Government of the Kingdom of the Netherlands, and of which a certified copy shall be sent, through diplomatic channels, to each of the States Members of the Hague Conference on Private International Law at the date of its Fourteenth Session.

APPENDIX 8:

THE U.S. DEPARTMENT OF STATE APPLICATION FOR ASSISTANCE UNDER THE HAGUE CONVENTION

UNITED STATES DEPARTMENT OF STATE
APPLICATION FOR ASSISTANCE UNDER THE HAGUE CONVENTION ON CHILD ABDUCTION
SEE PRIVACY STATEMENT ON REVERSE

OMB NO: 1405-0076
EXPIRES: 8-91
Estimated Burden – 1 Hour

I. IDENTITY OF CHILD AND PARENTS

CHILD'S NAME (LAST, FIRST, MIDDLE)	DATE OF BIRTH	PLACE OF BIRTH	
ADDRESS (Before removal)	U.S. SOCIAL SECURITY NO.	PASSPORT/IDENTITY CARD COUNTRY: NO.:	NATIONALITY
HEIGHT	WEIGHT	COLOR OF HAIR	COLOR OF EYES

FATHER / MOTHER

FATHER	MOTHER
NAME (Last, First, Middle)	NAME (Last, First, Middle)
DATE OF BIRTH / PLACE OF BIRTH	DATE OF BIRTH / PLACE OF BIRTH
NATIONALITY / OCCUPATION / PASSPORT/IDENTITY CARD COUNTRY: NO.:	NATIONALITY / OCCUPATION / PASSPORT/IDENTITY CARD COUNTRY: NO.:
CURRENT ADDRESS AND TELEPHONE NUMBER	CURRENT ADDRESS AND TELEPHONE NUMBER
U.S. SOCIAL SECURITY NO.	U.S. SOCIAL SECURITY NO.
COUNTRY OF HABITUAL RESIDENCE	COUNTRY OF HABITUAL RESIDENCE

DATE AND PLACE OF MARRIAGE AND DIVORCE, IF APPLICABLE

II. REQUESTING INDIVIDUAL OR INSTITUTION

NAME (Last, First, Middle)	NATIONALITY	OCCUPATION
CURRENT ADDRESS AND TELEPHONE NUMBER		PASSPORT/IDENTITY CARD COUNTRY: NO.:
COUNTRY OF HABITUAL RESIDENCE		
RELATIONSHIP TO CHILD	NAME, ADDRESS, AND TELEPHONE NO. OF LEGAL ADVISER, IF ANY	

III. INFORMATION CONCERNING THE PERSON ALLEGED TO HAVE WRONGFULLY REMOVED OR RETAINED CHILD

NAME (Last, First, Middle)		KNOWN ALIASES	
DATE OF BIRTH	PLACE OF BIRTH	NATIONALITY	
OCCUPATION, NAME AND ADDRESS OF EMPLOYER		PASSPORT/IDENTITY CARD COUNTRY: NO.:	U.S. SOCIAL SECURITY NO.
CURRENT LOCATION OR LAST KNOWN ADDRESS IN THE U.S.			
HEIGHT	WEIGHT	COLOR OF HAIR	COLOR OF EYES

FORM DSP-105
6-88

OTHER PERSONS WITH POSSIBLE ADDITIONAL INFORMATION RELATING TO THE WHEREABOUTS OF CHILD (Name, address, telephone number)

IV. TIME, PLACE, DATE, AND CIRCUMSTANCES OF THE WRONGFUL REMOVAL OR RETENTION

V. FACTUAL OR LEGAL GROUNDS JUSTIFYING THE REQUEST

VI. CIVIL PROCEEDINGS IN PROGRESS, IF ANY

VII. CHILD IS TO BE RETURNED TO:

NAME (Last, First, Middle)	DATE OF BIRTH	PLACE OF BIRTH
ADDRESS		TELEPHONE NUMBER

PROPOSED ARRANGEMENTS FOR RETURN TRAVEL OF CHILD

VIII. OTHER REMARKS

IX. DOCUMENTS ATTACHED (PREFERABLY CERTIFIED)

- ☐ DIVORCE DECREE
- ☐ CUSTODY DECREE
- ☐ PHOTOGRAPH OF CHILD
- ☐ OTHER AGREEMENT CONCERNING CUSTODY
- ☐ OTHER _____

SIGNATURE OF APPLICANT AND/OR STAMP OF CENTRAL AUTHORITY	DATE	PLACE

PRIVACY ACT STATEMENT

THIS INFORMATION IS REQUESTED UNDER THE AUTHORITY OF THE INTERNATIONAL CHILD ABDUCTION REMEDIES ACT, PUBLIC LAW 100-300. THE INFORMATION WILL BE USED FOR THE PURPOSE OF EVALUATING APPLICANTS' CLAIMS UNDER THE HAGUE CONVENTION ON THE CIVIL ASPECTS OF INTERNATIONAL CHILD ABDUCTION, LOCATING ABDUCTED CHILDREN, AND ADVISING APPLICANTS ABOUT AVAILABLE LEGAL REMEDIES. WITHOUT THE REQUESTED INFORMATION, U.S. AUTHORITIES MAY BE UNABLE EFFECTIVELY TO ASSIST IN LOCATING ABDUCTED CHILDREN.

Comments concerning the accuracy of the burden hour estimate on page 1 may be directed to OMB, OIRA, State Department Desk Officer, Wash., D.C. 20503

APPENDIX 9:

DIRECTORY OF CENTRAL AUTHORITIES OF THE HAGUE CONVENTION CONTRACTING STATES

NATION	ADDRESS
Argentina	Ministry of Foreign Relations, Legal Affairs Department, Reconquista 1088, Buenos Aires, Argentina
Australia	Commonwealth Central Authority, Attorney General's Department, National Circuit, Barton, A.C.T. 2600, Australia
Austria	Bundesministerium fur Justiz, Abteilung I 10, Postfach 63, A-1016 Vienna, Austria
Belize	Ministry of Social Services and Community Development, Belmopan, Belize
Burkina Faso	Le Ministre delegue charge de l'Action Sociale et de la Famille, 01 BP 515, Ouagadougou 01, Burkina Faso
Canada	Minister of Justice and Attorney General of Canada, Department of External Affairs, Tower C, 7th floor, Lester B. Pearson Building, 125 Sussex Drive, Ottawa, Ontario K1A 0G2, Canada
Denmark	Ministry of Justice, Department of Private Law, Aebelogade 1, 2100 Copenhagen 0, Denmark
Ecuador	Ministerio de Bienestar, Robles No. 850 y Avenida Amazonas, Quito, Ecuador
France	Le Ministere de la Justice, Bureau du droit Europeen et International eet de l'Entraide Judiciarire Internationale en matiere civile et commerciale, 57 rue St. Roch, 75001 Paris, France
Germany	Der Generalbundesanwalt beim, Bundesgerichtshof -Zentrale, Behorde nach dem Sorgerechts-ubereinkommens-Ausfuhrungsgesetz, Postfach 11 06 29, D-1000 Berlin 11
Hungary	The Ministry of Justice, Szalay utca 16, P.O. Box 54, 1363 Budapest, Hungary
Ireland	Department of Justice, 72-76 St. Stephen's green, Dublin 2, Ireland
Israel	The Attorney General, Ministry of Justice, P.O. Box 1087, Jerusalem 91010, Israel
Luxembourg	Le Procureur General d'Etat, Palais de Justice, Boite postale 15, L-2010 Luxembourg

Mexico	Ministry of Foreign Affairs, Juridical Consultancy, H omero 213, 16th Floor, Colonia Chapultepec-Morales, Mexico City 11570, Mexico
Monaco	Direction des Services Judiciaires, Palais de Justice, 5 rue Colonel Bellando de Castro, MC 98000, Monaco
New Zealand	The Secretary, Department of Justice, Private Box 180, Wellington, New Zealand
Norway	Justisdepartementet, Sivilavdelingen, 1 juridiske enhet, Postboks 8005 dep, 0030 Oslo 1, Norway
Netherlands	Ministerie van Justitie, Directie Staata - en Strafrecht, Afdelilng Internationale Rechtshulp, Schedeldoekshaven 100, Postbus 20301, 2500 EH THE HAGUE, Netherlands
Poland	Ministere de la Justice, Departement juridique, Al. Ujazdowskie 11, 00-950 Varsovie, Pologne
Portugal	Direcco-Geral dos Servicos, Tutelares de Menorees, Ministerio da Justica, Avenida Almirante Reis, 101, 1197 Lisboa Codex, Portugal
Romania	Ministere de la Justice, Bd. M. Kogalniceanu 33, Sector 5, Bucarest, Roumanie
Spain	Secretaria General Tecnica del Ministerio de Justicia, San Bernardo, 45, 28015 Madrid, Espagne
Sweden	Ministry for Foreign Affairs, Box 16121, 19323 Stockholm, Sweden
Switzerland	Office federal de la Justice, Autorite centrale en matiere d'enlevement international d'enfants, 3003 Berne, Suisse
United Kingdom	The Child Abduction Unit, Official Solicitors Department, 4th Floor, 81 Chancery Lane, London WC21 1DD, United Kingdom
United States of America	Office of Citizens Consular Services (CA/OCS/CCS), Room 4817, Department of State, Washington, D.C. 20520, United States of America

APPENDIX 10:

SAMPLE WILL CLAUSE APPOINTING A CUSTODIAN FOR MINOR CHILDREN

In the event that, upon my death, there is no living person who is entitled by law to the custody of my minor child or children, and who is available to assume such custody, I name my sister, MARY JONES, presently residing at [address], as legal guardian, to serve without bond, of such child. At this time, my only minor child is JOHN SMITH, born [Date of Birth].

APPENDIX 11:

TABLE OF STATE CHILD PORNOGRAPHY STATUTES

STATE	STATUTE
Alabama	Code of Alabama, §13-A-12-190
Alaska	Alaska Statutes, §11.41.455; 11.61.125
Arizona	Arizona Revised Statutes Annotated, §13-3552, et seq.
Arkansas	Arkansas Statutes Annotated, §41-4203, et seq.
California	California Penal Code, §311.2, et seq.
Colorado	§18-6-403, et seq.
Connecticut	Connecticut General Statutes Annotated, §53a-196a; 196b.
Delaware	Delaware Code Annotated, Title 11, §1108
District of Columbia	District of Columbia Code, §22-2011, et seq.
Florida	Florida Statutes Annotated, §827.071
Georgia	Code of Georgia, §26-9943a
Hawaii	Hawaii Revised Statutes, §707-750; 751
Idaho	Idaho Labor Code, §18-1507
Illinois	Illinois Revised Statutes, Chapter 38, §11-20.1; §3-6(c)
Indiana	Indiana Code Annotated, §35-42-4-4
Iowa	Code of Iowa, §728.12
Kansas	Kansas Statutes Annotated, §21-3516
Kentucky	Kentucky Revised Statutes, §531.300, et seq.
Louisiana	Louisiana Revised Statutes, §14:81.1
Maine	Maine Revised Statutes Annotated, Title 17, §2921, et seq.
Maryland	Maryland Annotated Code, Article 27, §419A
Massachusetts	Massachusetts Annotated Laws, Chapter 272, §29A, et seq.
Michigan	Michigan Statutes Annotated, §750.145c

Minnesota	Minnesota Statutes Annotated, §617.246, et seq.
Mississippi	Mississippi Code Annotated, §97-5-31, et seq.
Missouri	Annotated Missouri Statutes, §568.06, et seq.
Montana	Revised Montana Code Annotated, §45-5-625
Nebraska	Nebraska Revised Statutes, §28-1463, et seq.
New Hampshire	New Hampshire Revised Statutes Annotated, §649-A
New Jersey	New Jersey Revised Statutes Annotated, §2C:24-4
New Mexico	New Mexico Statutes Annotated, §0-6A-1, et seq.
New York	New York Penal Law, §263.00, et seq.
North Carolina	General Statutes of North Carolina, §14.190.13, et seq.
North Dakota	North Dakota Century Code, §12.1-27.2-01, et seq.
Ohio	Ohio Revised Code Annotated, §2907.321, et seq.
Oklahoma	Oklahoma Statutes Annotated, Title 21, §1021.2, et seq.
Oregon	Oregon Revised Statutes, §163.483, et seq.
Pennsylvania	Title 18, §6312
Rhode Island	Rhode Island General Laws, §11-9-1
South Carolina	South Carolina Code Annotated, §22-22-22, et seq.
Tennessee	Tennessee Code Annotated, §39-6-1137, et seq.
Texas	Texas Penal Code, §43.25, et seq.
Utah	Utah Code Annotated, §76-5a-1, et seq.
Vermont	Title 13, §2821, et seq.
Virginia	Code of Virginia Annotated, §18.2-374.1
Washington	Washington Revised Code, §9.68A.040, et seq.
West Virginia	West Virginia Code, §161-8C-1, et seq.
Wisconsin	Wisconsin Statutes Annotated, §940.203
Wyoming	Wyoming Statutes, §6-4-403

GLOSSARY

GLOSSARY

Abduction - The criminal or tortious act of taking and carrying away by force.

Abscond - To secrete oneself from the jurisdiction of the courts.

Acquiescence - Conduct that may imply consent.

Action at Law - A judicial proceeding whereby one party prosecutes another for a wrong done.

Actionable - Giving rise to a cause of action.

Adjudication - The determination of a controversy and pronouncement of judgment.

Adjudicatory Hearing - The process by which it is determined whether the allegations in a complaint can be proven and, if so, whether they fall within the jurisdictional categories of the juvenile court.

Admissible Evidence - Evidence which may be received by a trial court to assist the trier of fact, either the judge or jury, in deciding a dispute.

Adoption - Legal process pursuant to state statute in which a child's legal rights and duties toward his natural parent(s) are terminated, and similar rights and duties toward his adoptive parents are substituted.

Adversary - Opponent or litigant in a legal controversy or litigation.

Adversary Proceeding - A proceeding involving a real controversy contested by two opposing parties.

Answer - In a civil proceeding, the principal pleading on the part of the defendant in response to the plaintiff's complaint.

Appeal - Resort to a higher court for the purpose of obtaining a review of a lower court decision.

Appearance - To come into court, personally or through an attorney, after being summoned.

Appellate Court - A court having jurisdiction to review the law as applied to a prior determination of the same case.

Argument - A discourse set forth for the purpose of establishing one's position in a controversy.

Bastard - Children who are not born either in lawful wedlock or within a competent time after its termination.

Bench - The court and the judges composing the court collectively.

Burden of Proof - The duty of a party to substantiate an allegation or issue to convince the trier of fact as to the truth of their claim.

Caption - The heading of a legal document which contains the name of the court, the index number assigned to the matter, and the names of the parties.

Cause of Action - The factual basis for bringing a lawsuit.

Certiorari - A common law writ whereby a higher court requests a review of a lower court's records to determine whether any irregularities occurred in a particular proceeding.

Child Abuse - Any form of cruelty to a child's physical, moral or mental well-being.

Child Custody - The care, control and maintenance of a child which may be awarded by a court to one of the parents of the child.

Child Labor Laws - Network of laws on both federal and state levels, prescribing working conditions for children in terms of hours and nature of work which may be performed, all designed to protect the child.

Child Protective Agency - A state agency responsible for the investigation of child abuse and neglect reports.

Child Support - The legal obligation of parents to contribute to the economic maintenance of their children.

Child Welfare - A generic term which embraces the totality of measures necessary for a child's well being; physical, moral and mental.

Circumstantial Evidence - Indirect evidence by which a principal fact may be inferred.

Civil Action - An action maintained to protect a private, civil right as opposed to a criminal action.

Civil Court - The court designed to resolve disputes arising under the common law and civil statutes.

Civil Law - Law which applies to noncriminal actions.

Claimant - The party who brings the arbitration petition, also known as the plaintiff.

Clean Hands Doctrine - The concept that claimants who seek equitable relief must not themselves have indulged in any impropriety in relation to the transaction upon which relief is sought.

Complaint - In a civil proceeding, the first pleading of the plaintiff setting out the facts on which the claim for relief is based.

Compromise and Settlement - An arrangement arrived at, either in court or out of court, for settling a dispute upon what appears to the parties to be equitable terms.

Compulsory Education - The legal obligation to attend school up to a certain age.

Conciliation - The adjustment and settlement of a dispute in a friendly, unantagonistic manner.

Conclusion of Fact - A conclusion reached by natural inference and based solely on the facts presented.

Conclusion of Law - A conclusion reached through the application of rules of law.

Conclusive Evidence - Evidence which is incontrovertible.

Corporal Punishment - Physical punishment as distinguished from pecuniary punishment or a fine; any kind of punishment of, or inflicted on, the body.

Counterclaims - Counterdemands made by a respondent in his or her favor against a claimant.

Court - The branch of government responsible for the resolution of disputes arising under the laws of the government.

Cross-Claim - A claim litigated by co-defendants or co-plaintiffs against each other.

Cross-Examination - The questioning of a witness by someone other than the one who called the witness to the stand concerning matters about which the witness testified during direct examination.

Defendant - In a civil proceeding, the party responding to the complaint.

Defense - Opposition to the truth or validity of the plaintiff's claims.

Delinquent - An infant of not more than a specified age who has violated criminal laws or has engaged in disobedient, indecent or immoral conduct, and is in need of treatment, rehabilitation, or supervision.

Discovery - Modern pretrial procedure by which one party gains information held by another party.

Disposition - The process by which the juvenile court decides what is to be done with, for, or about the child who has been found to be within its jurisdiction.

Domicile - The one place designated as an individual's permanent home.

Due Process Rights - All rights which are of such fundamental importance as to require compliance with due process standards of fairness and justice.

Duty - The obligation, to which the law will give recognition and effect, to conform to a particular standard of conduct toward another.

Emancipation - The surrender of care, custody and earnings of a child, as well as renunciation of parental duties.

Expert Witness - A witness who has special knowledge about a certain subject, upon which he or she will testify, which knowledge is not normally possessed by the average person.

Eyewitness - A person who can testify about a matter because of his or her own presence at the time of the event.

Fact Finder - In a judicial or administrative proceeding, the person, or group of persons, that has the responsibility of determining the acts relevant to decide a controversy.

Fact Finding - A process by which parties present their evidence and make their arguments to a neutral person, who issues a nonbinding report based on the findings, which usually contains a recommendation for settlement.

GLOSSARY

Finding - Decisions made by the court on issues of fact or law.

Hearing - A proceeding during which evidence is taken for the purpose of determining the facts of a dispute and reaching a decision.

Illegitimacy - A child who is born at a time when his parents are not married to each other.

Illegitimate - Illegal or improper. Also used to describe the status of children born out of wedlock.

In Camera - Latin for "in chambers." Refers to proceedings held in the privacy of a judge's chambers.

In Loco Parentis - Latin for "in the place of a parent." Refers to an individual who assumes parental obligations and status without a formal, legal adoption.

Incapacity - Incapacity is a defense to breach of contract which refers to a lack of legal, physical or intellectual power to enter into a contract.

Incest - The crime of sexual intercourse or cohabitation between a man and woman who are related to each other within the degrees wherein marriage is prohibited by law.

Infancy - The period prior to reaching the legal age of majority.

Infancy Presumption - At common law, the conclusive presumption that children under the age of seven were without criminal capacity.

Judge - The individual who presides over a court, and whose function it is to determine controversies.

Judgment - A judgment is a final determination by a court of law concerning the rights of the parties to a lawsuit.

Jurisdiction - The power to hear and determine a case.

Jurisprudence - The study of legal systems and the law.

Juvenile Court - A court which has special jurisdiction, of a parental nature, over delinquent, dependent and neglected children.

Kidnapping - The illegal taking of a person against his or her will.

Legal Aid - A national organization established to provide legal services to those who are unable to afford private representation.

Legal Capacity - Referring to the legal capacity to sue, it is the requirement that a person bringing the lawsuit have a sound mind, be of lawful age, and be under no restraint or legal disability.

Minor - A person who has not yet reached the age of legal competence, which is designated as 18 in most states.

Oath - A sworn declaration of the truth under penalty of perjury.

Objection - The process by which it is asserted that a particular question, or piece of evidence, is improper, and it is requested that the court rule upon the objectionable matter.

Overrule - A holding in a particular case is overruled when the same court, or a higher court, in that jurisdiction, makes an opposite ruling in a subsequent case on the identical point of law ruled upon in the prior case.

Parens Patriae - Latin for "parent of his country." Refers to the role of the state as guardian of legally disabled individuals.

Parties - The disputants.

Paternity - The relationship of fatherhood.

Pendente Lite - Refers to matters that are pending until, and contingent upon, the outcome of the lawsuit.

Petitioner - One who presents a petition to a court or other body either in order to institute an equity proceeding or to take an appeal from a judgment.

Plaintiff - In a civil proceeding, the one who initially brings the lawsuit.

Pleadings - Refers to plaintiff's complaint which sets forth the facts of the cause of action, and defendant's answer which sets forth the responses and defenses to the allegations contained in the complaint.

Procreation - The generation of children.

Rape - The unlawful sexual intercourse with a female person without her consent.

GLOSSARY

Selective Emancipation - The doctrine under which a child is deemed emancipated for only a part of the period of minority, or from only a part of the parent's rights, or for some purposes, and not for others.

Separation Agreement - Written arrangements concerning custody, child support, spousal support, and property division usually made by a married couple who decide to live separate and apart in contemplation of divorce.

Service of Process - The delivery of legal court documents, such as a complaint, to the defendant.

Show Cause Order - An accelerated method of starting an action, brought on by motion, which compels the opponent to respond within a shorter time period than usual.

Single Parent Family - A family in which one parent remains the primary caretaker of the children, and the children maintain little or no contact with the other parent.

Status Offender - A child who commits an act which is not criminal in nature, but which nevertheless requires some sort of intervention and disciplinary attention merely because of the age of the offender.

Supreme Court - In most jurisdictions, the Supreme Court is the highest appellate court, including the federal court system.

Testify - The offering of a statement in a judicial proceeding, under oath and subject to the penalty of perjury.

Testimony - The sworn statement make by a witness in a judicial proceeding.

Trial - The judicial procedure whereby disputes are determined based on the presentation of issues of law and fact. Issues of fact are decided by the trier of fact, either the judge or jury, and issues of law are decided by the judge.

Trial Court - The court of original jurisdiction over a particular matter.

Truancy - Willful and unjustified failure to attend school by one who is required to attend.

Unconstitutional - Refers to a statute which conflicts with the United States Constitution rendering it void.

Unfit - Incompetent.

Uniform Laws - Laws that have been approved by the Commissioners on Uniform State Laws, and which are proposed to all state legislatures for consideration and adoption.

Visitation - The right of one parent to visit children of the marriage under order of the court.

Ward - A person over whom a guardian is appointed to manage his or her affairs.

Youthful Offender - An individual who is older than a juvenile but younger than an adult.

BIBLIOGRAPHY

BIBLIOGRAPHY

Ackerman, Marc J., *Clinician's Guide to Child Custody Evaluations.* New York, NY: John Wiley & Sons, Inc., 1995.

Atkinson, Jeff, *Handling Religious Issues in Custody and Visitation.* Chicago, IL: American Bar Association, 1992.

Black's Law Dictionary, Fifth Edition. St. Paul, MN: West Publishing Company, 1979.

International Child Abductions: A Guide to Applying the Hague Convention. Chicago, IL: American Bar Association, 1993.

Grandparent Visitation Disputes: A Legal Resource Manual. Chicago, IL: American Bar Association, 1989.

Guralnick, Mark S., *Interstate Child Custody Litigation.* Chicago, IL: American Bar Association, 1993.

Mason, Mary Ann, *From Father's Property to Children's Rights.* New York, NY: Columbia University Press, 1994.